Making Time to Write

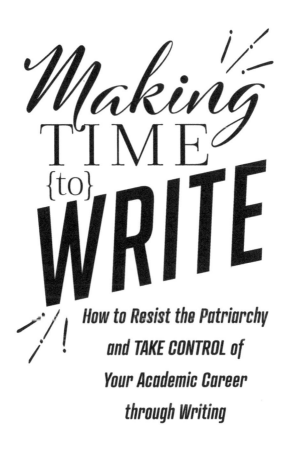

Making TIME {to} WRITE

How to Resist the Patriarchy and TAKE CONTROL of Your Academic Career through Writing

CATHY MAZAK, PhD

NEW YORK

LONDON • NASHVILLE • MELBOURNE • VANCOUVER

Making Time to Write

How to Resist the Patriarchy and Take Control of Your Academic Career Through Writing

Published in New York, New York, by Morgan James Publishing. Morgan James is a trademark of Morgan James, LLC. www.MorganJamesPublishing.com

Proudly distributed by Ingram Publisher Services.

Morgan James BOGO™

A **FREE** ebook edition is available for you or a friend with the purchase of this print book.

CLEARLY SIGN YOUR NAME ABOVE

Instructions to claim your free ebook edition:
1. Visit MorganJamesBOGO.com
2. Sign your name CLEARLY in the space above
3. Complete the form and submit a photo of this entire page
4. You or your friend can download the ebook to your preferred device

ISBN 9781631958212 paperback
ISBN 9781631958229 ebook
Library of Congress Control Number:
2021952423

Cover Design by:
Rachel Lopez
www.r2cdesign.com

Interior Design by:
Chris Treccani
www.3dogcreative.net

Morgan James PUBLISHING Builds with... Habitat for Humanity Peninsula and Greater Williamsburg

Morgan James is a proud partner of Habitat for Humanity Peninsula and Greater Williamsburg. Partners in building since 2006.

Get involved today! Visit MorganJamesPublishing.com/giving-back

Contents

Acknowledgments

I was afraid to write this book. Though I've published academic work before, I was afraid that I couldn't sustain a book-length work that was about my own ideas about writing (not my academic research). My friends laughed at me because, of course, every week for the past two years, I've released a podcast episode of me talking about writing. I guess I did have a lot to say, after all.

To my supportive academic coaching friends, Jane Jones, Sarah Dobson, and Kemi Doll ("The Boutique Mastermind"), for your unending encouragement, insight, and support every week for over a year. You are making many people's lives better through your work, including my own.

To Jane Jones and Kali Handelman, for their support in Jane's Elevate book coaching program. Jane is such an amazing coach that she can make a book breakthrough happen with one spot-on question. Kali is an outstanding developmental editor who always provided thoughtful and kindly worded feedback on this manuscript.

To Paula Diaco, who helped me get this book from an idea in my head to a submitted proposal with support, patience, and grace.

To Morgan James Publishing, for believing in this book and supporting it every step of the way. I'd especially like to thank Nick Pavlidis for getting my proposal in the right hands at Morgan James.

To my patient line editor, Aubrey Kosa, who waited (and waited and waited) while I finished this manuscript.

To the amazing team at Cathy Mazak, LLC, thank you so much for your encouragement and support. It is a joy to (virtually) go to work every day with all of you! Paulette Almodóvar-Arroyo, thank you for all the behind-the-scenes work you do to make everything run smoothly. Gina Robinson, Rocío Caballero-Gill, and Thea Racelis, you are absolutely the best coaches out there and our clients are so lucky to be supported by you. Yulia Denisyuk, I love every minute of working with you as a fellow writer and inspirational genius womxn.

To our clients, who were in my mind every moment of writing this book. Thank you for trusting me.

To LaToya Russell, who pushed me to just get started writing this book already! Thank you for being my business bestie.

To my dear children: Mariana, Guillermito, and Mariela. We were literally "locked down" together for the entire time I wrote this book, and even though some of you slammed through the door during my writing time

(Mariela!), you understood when I needed to be left alone to write. Mariana, thank you for the encouraging sticky notes I would find on my computer telling me how proud you are of me. I'm proud of you, too.

And finally, to the love of my life, Guillermo. I love you with all my heart. You've always, always supported even my wildest ideas, and I can never thank you enough for that. The writer in me honors the writer in you, and every day I'm thankful for the writers we've created together.

Part 1:

IT'S NOT YOU,
IT'S THE PATRIARCHY[1]

Chapter 1:

How Academia is Structured to Keep Womxn from Writing

If you picked up this book because making time to write is, and has always been, hard for you, hear this loud and clear.

It's not you. It's the patriarchy.[2]

Most books about writing focus on the behaviors that individuals can adopt to increase the number of words they put on the page per day or per week. Reading about strategies such as writing a minimum number of words per day, every day, might lead you to believe that writing is simply accomplished by *you* getting *your* act together. But that's not true.

Here's what I've found through my own journey on the tenure track to full professor, along with coaching hundreds of academic womxn and nonbinary people to write and publish more: the key to understanding why it's so hard to get your writing done is recognizing that the way the culture of academia is *organized* makes it hard for you. By feeling perpetually stressed out, by writing on nights and weekends because writing just does not fit into your workday, and by feeling guilty when you're not writing and overwhelmed when you are, you are behaving exactly how the racist, ableist patriarchy wants you to (or, as bell hooks would call it, the "imperialist white supremacist capitalist patriarchy").[3] If you continue on this path at the stress levels you are currently experiencing, you will either break down or burn out.

And that is precisely how the culture of academia is structured for womxn, nonbinary people, and anyone who doesn't "fit" into the stereotypical White male standard of the professorate.

Seeing how your individual struggles to write are connected to institutional and social structures is not blame-shifting. In fact, it is the only way to truly break out of the cycle of overwork and build a sustainable writing practice you actually enjoy. When you see how your individual actions support or disrupt the toxic, racist, sexist, ableist culture of academia, you make better everyday decisions, and you are more likely to make changes to your writing practices that really stick.

This book helps you see. It makes the connection between the culture of academia and your (in)ability to get writing done. Uncovering the connections between deeply ingrained cultural beliefs and the everyday choices we make when we sit down to write helps us make better choices—choices around writing that can be powerful acts of resistance. Imagine the power behind a professorate full of womxn and nonbinary people who can say "no" to projects that don't move their careers forward, who have a thriving, positive relationship with their writing so that writing energizes them instead of causing them self-doubt. Imagine the power of womxn and nonbinary academics who are well-rested and have space to think, and how that simple (not easy, but simple) shift could change knowledge-making.

If you can quiet that nagging voice in your head that makes you think you can't say "no," that is driven by scarcity and fear, and step into your power by doing the work this book calls you to do, you will not only change your writing practice but also your life, your career, and your relationship to academia.

Don't get me wrong: it is not your responsibility to change the culture of academia. Change to the structure of oppression absolutely must happen, but that sort of structural change is not the focus of this book. The kind of change I'm seeking to ignite is a change inside of *you*—a change that makes you happier, less stressed, and more prolific. I deeply believe that individual change has a ripple effect that will add up to a cultural shift, but hear this clearly: changing yourself and how you experience academia is enough. And that is also the mission of this book.

Who This Book is For

This book is for academic womxn and nonbinary people. As those words can mean different things to different people, I will briefly define what I mean.

I use "academic" to refer to graduate students, faculty members (part- or full-time, contingent or tenure track), and researchers. I'm choosing to use the term womxn to align with the work of intersectional feminists and signal the inclusion of Black, Indigenous, and people of color.[4] I include nonbinary people to acknowledge that gender is a spectrum, and by only talking about "womxn" and "men," I would be reinforcing a false (and patriarchal) binary. I use womxn "to recognize the agency of womxn, individually and collectively, and to challenge the notion that womxn are necessarily defined through their relation to men."[5] I'm aware that language is ever-changing and the spelling of womxn-with-an-x may mean something different in other contexts over time. I'm making the somewhat risky choice to go with that spelling anyway, standing on its origins and "herstory," as I attempt to forge meaning.

Many of the stories and pieces of advice in this book connect the particular socialization of womxn in North American culture into the culture of academia. This is key to how I approach the mindset work and the day-to-day strategies laid out in this book. Because of this, I use the term womxn to include "anyone who has ever, ever will, or currently identifies as a womxn."[6] That is, I'm writing this book for every womxn in academia, socialized or identifying, and for all nonbinary academics. How your body and your gender identity are read by the institutions where you study and work affects the way you interact with those institutions, as does the socialization of womxn and nonbinary people in the racist, ableist patriarchy. Understanding the interaction of an individual with social structures is at the foundation of making time to write in academia but is rarely acknowledged or explained.

An Institution That Was Not Built for You

Institutions of higher education were not intended for womxn and nonbinary people. In the colonial United States, womxn were not legally allowed to attend college. By 1860, there were some institutions that granted degrees to White womxn, but they were limited to a subset of the degrees offered to White men. The idea that only certain programs of study were appropriate for womxn, African Americans, Native Americans, and other minoritized groups was predominant until as late as the 1970s.

Higher education's role in reproducing social inequalities has long been clear and is accepted among many academics as a "sad but true" fact of life (often with a shoulder shrug). Tech companies invest in programs to solve the "pipeline problem," referring to the paucity of Black, Indigenous, and Latinx graduates who are trained to start tech careers. Likewise, STEM education focuses on trying to increase the number of womxn in "hard sciences."

Campuses are becoming more and more racially and socio-economically diverse, yet universities are slow to respond in a way that makes minoritized students feel welcome.[7] The structure of academia actually replicates the "diversity problem." Minoritized students' interactions with mostly White, male professors will reinforce the idea that the university is not a place for them, and they may not pursue graduate degrees as a result. Fewer graduate students who are womxn, nonbinary, Black, Indigenous, Latinx, or people of color lead to gender and race gaps in the professorate. According to catalyst.org, in the United States, Canada, Australia, and Europe, the higher up the academic ladder you go, the wider the gender gap. In the United States, womxn are less likely than men to be granted tenure. Womxn of color are even more underrepresented in academia with Black, Hispanic, Pacific Islander, American Indian/Alaska Native womxn totaling just 6 percent of full-time faculty—combined.[8] By the time you look at the highest rank (with the highest paychecks)—full professors—womxn and minority groups are *even more* underrepresented.[9]

As if that's not bad enough, across the board professors who are men earn more than womxn professors at all ranks. In fact, the gender wage gap in academia closely mirrors the gender wage gap across all professions, despite academia's supposed liberal bent. Womxn in academia make 81.6 cents on the dollar to men (And, to be clear, this statistic is pretty much referring to White women and White men). Ten years ago, womxn made 80.8 cents on the dollar. But the total number of womxn in faculty positions grew by 24 percent in ten years, making womxn 44.8 percent of full-time faculty.[10] These numbers lump together womxn of all races. The disparities for Black womxn, Indigenous womxn, and womxn of color are much greater.

As in many other aspects of society, womxn and non-binary people have had to fight their way into male-dominated academic spaces. Once there, they are expected to conform to cultural norms that were created by and for men. For example, womxn are still told not to have children during their graduate studies and early careers. Advisors can push pregnant students out of programs by cutting or reducing funding, as Jessica Smartt Gullion recounted in her chapter of *Mama, PhD*.[11] If the "traditional" path through academia is understood as one where students are single during their graduate studies and delay (or avoid) caregiving responsibilities until after they have tenure, then the "traditional" path is leaving a lot of people out.

I have had three children during my time on the tenure track. When I came back from my first maternity leave, a senior male colleague pulled me aside after a faculty meeting to tell me that it was not fair that I got "vacation" and that he would also be able to write more if he could take so much time "off." After baby number three, when I had become really good at controlling my pipeline and making time to write, a senior female colleague pulled me aside and asked if I had used my maternity leave to finish my book when, in fact, I had manipulated my pipeline so that my maternity leave fell in the window between the final submission of revised publications (In this case, they were two coedited volumes and a coauthored article in a top-tier journal.) and when they would officially be published. This was a very deliberate choice on my part because I wanted to be 100 percent focused on the baby during my maternity leave—not trying to polish almost-done projects while sleep-deprived. The result was that all those publications came out the semester I returned from maternity.

This, apparently, was unbelievable to my colleagues. But that's because having a childbearing body is unbelievable in the academic context. To succeed, the culture of academia says you must act like a childless (or child-ignoring) male. Thus, the "traditional" path. Thus, the disbelief that anyone could develop systems and practices that would allow them to actually take time off for months to have a baby. Thus, pushing out pregnant and breastfeeding bodies. How could those bodies focus on scholarly work?

The very definition of how one goes about focusing on scholarly work is highly patriarchal. It's racist, too. The hashtag #blackintheivory, created by Joy Melody Woods as she tweeted with Shardé M. Davis, shares horror stories of racist treatment in academia.[12] Entire organizations such as The Cite Black Women Collective were created to counteract the racist, patriarchal culture of academia that is structured to continually push Black and Indigenous people and people of color out in impactful ways, such as through citation politics.[13] It is well-documented that student evaluations are biased against womxn, particularly against Black womxn. Since many of the founding institutions of higher education in the United States were literally built by enslaved people or the excess capital made possible by slavery, the fact that womxn, nonbinary, and BIPOC scholars face structural biases that make it less likely they'll receive full professorship should come as no surprise. The pressure to compete inside of structures rigged to favor White men shapes the experiences of womxn and nonbinary people in academia.

The University Embedded in Fast Capitalism

Higher education believes it exists outside—actually, above—global economies. Of course, higher education is as entrenched in global fast capitalism as Microsoft and Facebook. Huge budget cuts to state institutions (e.g., University of Alaska, University of Illinois) and the beginning of the end of the tenure system (e.g., University of Wisconsin) are just two clues that higher education is severely affected by late-stage capitalism. This shows up most glaringly when we look at the changes in higher education's workforce in the past fifteen years. The exploitation of contingent faculty, overproduction of graduate students entering flooded markets, and squeezing of every ounce of "productivity" out of faculty are all in line with what is happening in other industries.[14] There are fewer staff members, meaning faculty must take on excess admin burden, but because of flooded markets, the performance of faculty in research, teaching, and service is expected to go up, and up, and up. Contingent faculty live paycheck to paycheck without the stability of a contract more than a few months long and are barely piecing together a full-time income by teaching on multiple campuses.

The effects of late-stage capitalism on universities and colleges should not come as a surprise, since these institutions played a pivotal role in supporting early capitalism and European American colonialism "through their consolidation and propagation of racialized ideologies."[15] Early US institutions of higher education were built by the labor of enslaved people or with money from slaveholders and went on to propagate pseudoscientific "proof" to support racial inequalities. So, to say that academia played a role in ensuring that racial inequality is woven into the fabric of American life and economy would be putting it mildly.

Thinking about how to dismantle the structural inequalities inside academia, which are so deeply woven into economies and communities at every level, is absolutely overwhelming. But if we can tap on a crack in the foundation of it all, maybe we can bring the structure down, one individual at a time. That's where writing comes in. Publishing is the capital of academia. To address the problem of womxn and nonbinary people, and especially womxn and nonbinary people of color, not getting equal representation in the professorate (particularly at the full professor level), we need to address their writing problem.

Womxn write less not because they have less to say but because they have less time to write than their male counterparts. An article in *Inside Higher Ed* reported that top journals saw submission by womxn tank during the COVID-

19 lockdown.[16] An open letter from Andrea R. Jain, editor of Journal of the American Academy of Religion, laments that "submissions by women dropped, although the number of submissions to the *JAAR* remained steady. I am not exaggerating when I say that almost all of the article submissions I have received in the time of the pandemic have come from men.[17]" Womxn were already taking on a greater service burden in their departments; they were also picking up the care burden dropped when schools closed during the pandemic.[18] The COVID-19 global pandemic exacerbated existing problems within higher education. The consequences of universities intentionally designing themselves as cogs in the fast-capitalist gears have exploded into plain view. Furloughs, firings, department closings, whole university closings all seemed justified when the lockdown caused the US economy to tank. If there were disparities in the professorate based on race and gender before, they became even more salient during the pandemic.

The writing problems of womxn and nonbinary academics are the result of social inequalities compounded by a problem all academics face. In 2017, Maggie Berg and Barbara K. Seeber published *The Slow Professor: Challenging the Culture of Speed in the Academy*, in which they lay out exactly how academic labor is like all fast-capitalist labor: overworked, dripping in minutiae, silenced, and obedient. But these characteristics of fast-capitalist labor are actually exacerbated by academia's cultural beliefs and expectations. "[T]he long-standing perception of professors as a leisured class has produced a defensive culture of guilt and overwork ... flexibility of hours can translate into work-ing all the time, particularly because academic work by its very nature is never done."[19] Add antiacademic sentiments unleashed by the Trump administration and academics are working themselves into the ground simply to have their work dismissed as leftist conspiracy.

Cal Newport's popular 2016 book, *Deep Work*, con-nected the plight that many academics feel to cultural trends within white-collar workplaces that glorify over-work and revel in minutiae. He argues that we don't have time to do our real work—the deep work of developing thoughts and ideas—because we are overly connected by technology, expected to respond to every email within minutes, and taxed by the unimportant but urgent (he calls this "the shallows"). Newport wrote a book that res-onated with anyone who feels like they "run their day out of their inbox," but his insights come from a career as a computer science professor. Newport's advice for getting out of "the shallows" and into the deep work has been criticized as being steeped in male privilege. Advice such as "become hard to reach" seems, well, easier to implement for White males. In academia, womxn take on more of a service burden, find it harder to say "no" for fear of seem-ing uncooperative, and have had to fight their way into institutions not created for them.

The consequences of the fast-capitalist university fall more heavily on those who have been marginalized in aca-demia from the start: womxn, members of the LGBTQ community, BIPOC scholars, and those with disabilities or chronic illness. Berg and Seeber acknowledge the rejection of non-White-male-abled-bodies in academia when they say, "to talk about the body and emotion goes against the grain of an institution that privileges the mind and reason."[20]

Universities have been operating under an unsustainable model (just as all fast capitalism and racist, ableist heteropatriarchy is unsustainable). As the old ways of being in academia crumble, we have the opportunity to remake the university in our image. Academia *must* be remade to be more inclusive and equitable. Although the institutionalized racism and sexism baked into the structures of academic institutions must be dismantled, the most immediate way to influence this remaking is at the grass-roots level, at the level of individual faculty members. This is the conclusion Berg and Seeber make after their review of literature about the corporate university: "A surprisingly common thread ... is an emphasis on change being in the hands of individual professors."[21] And for this reason, Berg and Seeber "see individual practice as a site of resistance," and so do I.

Writing as Resistance

There are two ways to create a thriving writing practice. The way the racist, ableist patriarchy wants you to do it is by working nights and weekends, feeling guilty when you're not working, saying "yes" to everything out of fear and desperation, basically ignoring your health and the possibility of the deep contribution to your field a rested you would make. This is the path many of us take. If you have been trying to keep up with the demands of academia this way, I know you are doing the best you can with the training you got—no judgment here. But don't be fooled: this is a path that upholds the patriarchy. This is a path that continues to marginalize womxn, nonbinary people, people of color, caretakers, people with chronic conditions, the neurodiverse, really anyone who does not fit the accepted academic mold.

The second way to create a thriving writing practice is to see your writing as an act of resistance to the racist, ableist patriarchy. This kind of writing practice centers your relationship with writing. It involves a twofold shift: mindset and writing as an activity. Your writing practice must center *you*: your career and big goals, your rest and restoration, your boundaries around your time. When you make time to write, enjoy writing, and think of it as *the* work (instead of a by-product of the work), you are pushing back on the culture of overwork, the glorification of busy, and the patriarchal expectations around how you are supposed to act as a womxn or nonbinary person in academia. This book seeks to help you build such a practice.

Rebellious Reflections

In each chapter, I'll include some reflective prompts to help you process the information. Taking the time to reflect on yourself and your work is absolutely patriarchy-disrupting.

I've compiled these questions in a free, fillable PDF workbook for you, along with additional exercises that flesh out the main points of each chapter through more reflective action. You can get the free workbook by going to my website: https://www.cathymazak.com/workbook.

1. What does the "culture of overwork" look like at your institution?

2. How do you and/or your colleagues "glorify busy"?

3. What would happen if you stopped working nights and weekends?

4. How would you describe your relationship with your writing right now?

Chapter 2:
The Danger of the Twin Scarcities

The number one reason academic womxn and non-binary people give for letting writing fall to the bottom of their list is lack of time. In my past five years as a writing coach, I've heard hundreds of my clients say that they know they need to "make time to write," but they haven't been able to. Of course, the time we have is the time we have; we can't "make" additional time, despite attempts to wake up earlier and stay up later. The obstacles that we face around writing, then, are attached to the way we perceive time. We continually bump up against the "no time" problem because academia conditions us for scarcity.

Academic culture thrives on the twin scarcities: lack of time and lack of money. From the moment we enter our doctoral programs, we are conditioned for scarcity. By being paid a low "stipend" and expected to work twenty-four seven, we are ingrained with the belief that there is never enough time or money in academia. Imagine any other job that requires a bachelor's degree and pays less than $20,000 per year for the privilege to work *all the time*. Assistantships are competitive (again, scarcity), and so we should just be really happy to get one because we (usually) don't have to pay tuition. And tuition is very, very expensive (again, money is scarce).

When I met my husband Guillermo at Michigan State in the early 2000s, I was teaching in the intensive English program and he was a new doctoral student in animal science (No, he was not my student ... okay, his sister was my student, but we started dating *after* she finished my class). I was making $24,000 a year working full-time teaching with my master's degree.

After I decided to leave that position to pursue my PhD in Critical Studies in the Teaching of English, I was "lucky" to receive a teaching assistantship. I question the term "lucky" because the idea that assistantships are highly competitive is the beginning of the scarcity narrative in academia. That narrative is so strong and so ingrained that I felt "lucky" to be able to leave my $24,000 a year job to be paid $12,000 a year and have my tuition covered.

Now, considering the cost of tuition at Michigan State and the number of courses I was teaching (two instead of four), this seemed like a great deal on paper—a step up, even. But it's really, really hard to live in the United

States on $12,000 a year (as many of you reading this book know).

I made it work by using credit cards.

And so began a narrative in my own head about how there is never enough money and I would always be in the hole. This narrative started in graduate school but continues to this day.

Next to my $12,000 a year, Guillermo's $18,000 a year, delivered as a combination of stipend and assistantship, seemed luxurious. But of course, it wasn't. The big pay grade difference bought him a job that chained him to the lab day and night. He studied fat cells in a dish, so those cells needed to be kept alive for his lab to function. He had to feed them, photograph them, count them—and cells don't sleep. I vividly remember midnight walks in below-zero Michigan winters to accompany him to the lab to feed the cells.

The twin scarcities of time and money are inextricably linked. In addition to scarcity around money (because living on $18,000 isn't so easy either), grad school ingrained in Guillermo the belief of scarcity around time. And, perhaps more toxically, it instilled in him the belief that academic work can happen at any time of day or night. There are no boundaries. The work requires us twenty-four seven.

Once you're out of graduate school and into more steady work, the twin scarcities don't magically go away. For me and Guillermo, they followed us onto the tenure track. Student loan debt made it difficult for us to establish a household and buy a car, all while we considered ourselves so, so lucky to have landed tenure-track jobs at the same university. We got pregnant with our first baby by surprise in those very early tenure-track years, and while I struggled to fit my academic work into daycare hours, Guillermo, conditioned by lab work that required him twenty-four seven, let work flow into our nights and weekends. Pushing back on this overwork was extra hard pretenure when we were both worried that one wrong move would mean we would lose our miracle dual-tenure-track positions.

But even after we both earned tenure, the twin scarcities often drove our career decision-making. And that's the real problem: when you operate from a place of scarcity, you make choices based on fear. Fear is a powerful motivator, but choices based in fear often have the opposite effect of what you intend. If you take on too many writing projects based on fear that you won't have enough publications, your pipeline will slow down to a trickle. If you don't put up boundaries around your writing time because you fear angering people on your tenure committee, you'll never build a healthy writing practice. The purpose of this chapter is to help you recognize and then unlearn scarcity mindset so that you can stop making choices based on fear and step into choices based on abundance. This mindset shift is about the creation of an abundance framework within which to make decisions, both in your day-to-day academic life and in key inflection points in your career.

Unlearning Scarcity Mindset

Your ability to make decisions is rooted in your mindset, and mindset is your set of beliefs about something that drives your behavior. Your mindset is heavily influenced by both the way you were socialized and your experiences in academia. As we learn more about scarcity mindset and the role it has been playing in your writing practice, our goal is to shift from scarcity to abundance.

On one hand, scarcity mindset tells us there is never enough, that we must hold on to resources with a death grip. Scarcity stokes our worst fears of failure. On the other hand, abundance mindset tells us that there are plenty of opportunities, that we can make choices from a place of power and intentionality. Abundance makes room for success on your terms. Scarcity keeps us saying "yes" to writing projects that don't really align with what we're trying to accomplish in our careers just to get a publication. Abundance mindset leads to a curated pipeline, where only the best, most impactful writing projects are worthy of your attention.

Understanding how you learned a scarcity mindset for time and money is the first step in changing that mindset to one of abundance. This change is hard, and it takes time and self-reflection to make. In the free workbook that accompanies this book, available at https://www.cathy-mazak.com/workbook, I walk you through additional exercises to guide you through the process. It's so difficult to reject scarcity mindset because, in some ways, that mindset has served us well. Maybe a belief in scarcity has prompted you to aggressively pursue grant funding and this has quite literally paid off for you. Maybe your beliefs around the scarcity of time prompted you to learn time management skills that have served you well. We must acknowledge how scarcity mindset has served us personally before we can release it.

As you work to shift your mindset from scarcity toward abundance, please know that the decisions you made based on scarcity and fear were perfectly rational decisions in the moment. They made total sense, and again, those choices probably served you well up to a point. However, your beliefs about the scarcity of time and money serve your institution(s) and the culture of academia much more than they serve you. To make time to write, you'll need to shift into an abundance mindset.

Rebellious Reflections

1. What practices or habits have you developed to save time?
2. What do you fear will happen if you run out of time to get your work done?
3. What choices have you made in your academic career to save money or make extra money?
4. What do you fear will happen if you don't bring in money?

Scarcity mindset keeps us in a place of fear. And this fear fuels all that is bad about the racist, ableist, patriarchal culture of academia. The ingrained scarcity of money keeps us from stepping fully into what we are creating as scholars pretenure because we fear losing our precious—and scarce—tenure track position. The fear of losing what little we have is a powerful driver for us to not rock the boat; therefore, making less impactful change. By keeping you operating from a place of fear with a scarcity mindset, your institution maintains the status quo—the status quo that relies on exploiting grad student labor and contingent faculty, the one that keeps faculties from unionizing, the one that continues to squeeze every ounce of work out of you at every hour of the day.

Now, let me be clear: I am NOT saying that an abundance mindset will magically line your pockets with money or change your institution's fast-capitalist policies. You cannot think your way to a million dollars! What I am saying is that to change how we interact with the culture of academia we need to change how we think. Is a scarcity mindset about money stopping you from fully realizing yourself as a scholar? Is fear of losing money causing you to make choices that are damaging your career—and maybe your mental health?

Let's dig into some of the ways that scarcity mindset about money in academia manifests itself and how we can push back by developing a mindset of abundance. As we look at examples, we'll be able to pick apart the important difference between a scarcity *mindset* and *actual* scarcity. Both are real, both are true, but you can do a lot more to change the scarcity mindset, which can help turn actual scarcity around or prevent it altogether.

The job market, for example, is a place where actual scarcity triggers scarcity mindset. The job market for PhDs in humanities is notoriously flooded. According to the *New York Times*, the number of tenure-track jobs for English professors has declined every year since 2012, for a total loss of 33 percent.[22] The result of this very real scarcity of tenure-track jobs for PhDs in humanities leads to a scarcity mindset *even if you already have a tenure-track job in humanities*. I was coaching a woman on the tenure track in French at a prestigious Ivy League institution. She had a low teaching load, support to do her writing and research, and a small child. She was considering having another baby but had been told by multiple members of her department that she should not do that pretenure.

"I'm just so lucky to have this job," she said, "I don't want to mess it up. So many of my brilliant colleagues from grad school are scraping by as adjuncts. If I'm being warned to not have a baby until after tenure, maybe I should heed those warnings."

Whoa. Stop. This is a scarcity mindset rearing its ugly head.

When we are successful at something that other people also want to achieve, and those other people are also talented and worthy of achieving it, a scarcity mindset tells us that we better not make a wrong move or we'll lose this precious thing that we probably only got by accident (my client literally described getting her job as a "crap shoot").

So, I asked her, "Can't it be true that you are talented and deserving of your tenure-track position *and* that your friends are talented and deserving of tenure-track positions, even if they don't have one?"

It was hard for her to process this false dichotomy because scarcity was so ingrained. But it is simultaneously true that:

- The market for humanities PhDs is flooded, and tenure-track jobs are hard to come by.
- There are many talented humanities PhDs without secure work.
- My client is a talented professor and worthy of her tenure-track line in humanities.

After talking about it more, she was able to come around—tentatively—to the idea that she was indeed qualified for her position.

Now, this particular client was a White womxn, so did structural inequities favor her in her degree and job pursuits? Yes, absolutely. As a White person, she has benefitted from structural racism. Does that mean that she should squash her plans for a second baby out of fear of losing tenure? No. It actually means that she is less likely to lose credibility in her department by getting pregnant because she is White.

Here is where *real scarcity* (a lack of jobs for PhDs in humanities) rubs up against a *scarcity mindset* and makes that scarcity mindset seem like a trusted way to make decisions when it is not.

Now let's look at an example of how scarcity mindset about time manifests itself in academia. It is true that time is limited. There are only twenty-four hours in a day, seven days in a week, and 365 days in a year. My first job out of college was working as a technical writer for a software company in Ann Arbor, Michigan. Picture a small, windowless office space, lines of cubicles, with everything corporate gray. After spending my undergrad in Bloomington, Indiana, reading books and walking through a beautiful, tree-filled campus every day, sitting in a cubicle for eight hours a day felt like torture. Imagining putting up with the cubicle life for thirty years was a big factor in my decision to go to grad school.

When I was thinking about life as an academic, one of the perks I thought about was that working hours seemed to be "flexible." Observing my professors, I could see that they taught evening classes, were rarely in their offices, and got to travel to conferences in interesting cities. Look at that flexibility! They were not chained to their desks! And indeed, we are not bound to the desk.

But, even worse, we are bound to the work.

And the work, for many of us, can happen at any time of day (or as my husband learned in his grad school lab, any time of night). Because we technically can work at any time, day or night, we are particularly vulnerable to the effects of late-stage capitalism on the university.

The University of Puerto Rico (UPR), where I became a tenured, full professor, is a clear example. Puerto Rico is a colony of the United States where the negative effects of late-stage capitalism are abundantly clear. Without getting into a modern history of Puerto Rico under US rule, let's just say that in 2016, the federal PROMESA law installed an unelected fiscal control board over the locally elected government whose mission it is to "restructure" Puerto Rico's debt. Part of this "restructuring" included a five-hundred-million-dollar cut to Puerto Rico's only public institution of higher education, the UPR system (Lest you think that cuts this deep are only happening in Puerto Rico, please reference the University of Alaska and University of Illinois for similar huge funding cuts).

In response to the cut, the university began to enact a series of policies that increasingly squeezed faculty in terms of time (it squeezed nonfaculty as well, but I'll use faculty examples here). First, sabbaticals were cut. Where before a professor could apply for a sabbatical to write a book or to do research in a library or lab outside of Puerto Rico, we no longer could. So you'd have to write your book during the academic year while you were teaching your 4-4 load or during the summer when you're technically not getting paid.

When I started as a UPR professor, I could get course release time just for writing grants (not even getting them!) to help encourage research and the pursuit of external funds in a university that required teaching four classes per semester for tenure-track faculty.

As the years went by, course releases for seeking grants were eliminated, and you could only get course releases to run grant-funded projects. Today, the policy is that you have to buy out your salary to release your time, which is prohibited in many grants programs (including the federal programs I had tapped for funding). You can get a grant (no matter what size), but you need to run it on your own time while teaching your 4-4 load, unless you can buy out your salary.

And external funding is just one example.

Administrative work, which used to come with course release time, also has to happen on top of your 4-4. This particular change took place while I was directing our graduate program, so I took on the role thinking I had reduced my load to 3-3 in order to run the graduate program, but the course release was taken away after just one semester, and I was expected to do the same administrative work without the course release.

So. We are squeezed. Expected to do the same amount of work—or more—in less time. And I'm sure you can think of a similar cut or policy change in your context that has led you to have to take on something more in your already overpacked schedule.

The way many people deal with this extra work is by working more hours. That's how we end up with sixty- to eighty-hour workweeks, as tasks that used to fit into the central "working hours" of our day must bleed into nights and weekends if we are to get everything done. This real addition of work to our responsibilities only feeds our scarcity mindset about time.

Scarcity Mindset and Writing

Now that we've established what scarcity mindset is and how it deeply affects academics and their beliefs about time and money, I want to dig into how scarcity mindset specifically affects our writing.

Since publications are the currency of academia, it's no surprise that like money scarcity, academic culture ingrains publication scarcity from the very start. But the way we are socialized in regard to the number of publications we have to publish is even more insidious than our socialization about the scarcity of time and money. The number of publications needed to get a job, get tenure, get full, get a grant—all of it is kept purposefully mysterious. How many publications are enough?

We never know.

Because we never know how much is enough, we believe that more is better. This belief reflects scarcity mindset and comes from a place of fear, and this fear of not having enough publications incites us to make decisions that actually cause us to publish *less*.

Picture the image of a pipeline: it is equal in diameter throughout its length. In theory, what flows in also flows out, but scarcity mindset has turned your publication pipeline into a funnel. Many projects get stuffed in the top, but only a few projects drip out the bottom—slowly. Fear driven by scarcity mindset causes you to make decisions about what goes into your publication pipeline, and those decisions end up having the opposite effect of what you intended. You are preventing publication abundance by operating from a scarcity mindset. By unlearning scarcity mindset, you can stop making decisions based on fear and start creating abundance in your writing.

I was coaching a client who was committed to a coauthored article that she really didn't want to work on. The topic was a little bit out of her main research area, so her own publications always got her energy and time because she felt confident and happy working on those. Every time we had a coaching call, she would express her guilt and overwhelm around this coauthored project.

"I just need to schedule it in and make myself do it because I really need that publication for tenure," she lamented.

I asked, "Do you really, though?"

We proceeded to list all the work she was excited about in her publication pipeline, and I said, "You've got a lot of publications here. Why do you keep putting time and energy into planning (and not writing) this particular coauthored one?"

She paused. She didn't need that coauthored article to have enough publications for tenure, but she had been operating with such a scarcity mindset around publications that she couldn't see when she had enough. We made a plan for her to back out of the coauthored publication (there was a lot of mindset work to do around that, too), and during our next call she was a different person.

"Getting rid of this project is such a weight lifted! I'm so much further ahead on everything else now that I released that project that was weighing me down, and my coauthors actually seemed kind of happy that I backed out!"

Like my client and her coauthoring project, you are holding onto writing projects that you don't love out of the fear that scarcity mindset generates. Below is a pipeline exercise that I've also included in the free PDF workbook, which you can get at: https://www.cathymazak.com/workbook.

Take a moment to imagine your publication pipeline—all the publications that you have currently in play, from idea to revisions and resubmits. Now put a mental gold star next to only those publications that bring you a surge of excitement and energy when you think about them. I know it is not realistic—or even smart—to release ALL of the projects that don't have a gold star, but I want you to imagine a world where the gold-star projects are enough. You are imagining abundance! And if you can overcome (or unlearn) your scarcity mindset, you can create that abundant world. Most of the clients I work with could be publishing more if their pipelines were less packed to the gills with projects that they just took on to get a publication.

The strategy to "just publish anything" actually makes you less likely to get a job, tenure, or full because you create a body of work that is disparate and confusing.

By packing your pipeline to the gills with projects outside of your gold-star projects, you also create a pipeline that moves more slowly because it is weighed down by an excess of projects. Because writing is the currency of academia, the twin scarcities combine to incite fear around writing. You must publish more, because if you don't, you won't get that job/promotion, thus losing already scarce financial resources; yet, your time is so squeezed that you can't fit writing in. The twin scarcities form the perfect storm for creating a funnel (with tons of writing projects shoved into the top) instead of a pipeline (with curated publications flowing out at a steady pace). The twin scarcities have been preventing publication abundance. By unlearning scarcity mindset, you can stop making decisions based on fear and start creating abundance in your writing.

Rebellious Reflections

1. What writing projects are weighing you down?
2. How could eliminating those weighty projects from your pipeline help you finish other publications faster?
3. What is scary about eliminating projects from your pipeline? In other words, what will actually happen if you decide to cut a writing project from your pipeline?

Stepping into Abundance

Now that you've identified some specific ways your mindset around the scarcity of money, time, and publications in academia is not serving you, it's time to replace scarcity mindset with an abundance mindset.

First, know this: changing your mindset is an act of resistance. If you identify as a womxn or have ever been socialized as one, believing that there is enough money, time, and publications for you to accomplish your deepest dreams is an absolutely revolutionary act.

Believing that YOU are enough is the greatest rebellion of all.

It's a big move, but you can do it.

Cultivating an abundance mindset starts with the work you've done so far in this chapter: recognizing how you've been conditioned for scarcity and have operated out of fear. Fear-based decisions feel safe. You are avoiding what's scary, so you are playing small. It's time for you to play big.

In *Playing Big: Practical Wisdom for Women Who Want to Speak Up, Create, and Lead*, Tara Mohr distinguishes between two types of fear based on the teaching of Rabbi Alan Lew. The first type of fear, *Pachad*, is the "overreactive, irrational fear that stems from worries about what *could* happen, about the worst-case scenarios we *imagine*."[23] The second type of fear, *Yirah*, is the fear that "overcomes us when we inhabit a larger space than we are used to [or] come into considerably more energy than we had before. It is what we feel in the presence of the divine."[24] Pachad is worry-fear. Yirah is excitement-fear.

A scarcity mindset thrives on worry-fear. Is it possible that you speaking up in a department meeting will turn certain colleagues against you and they will try to block you getting tenure? Yes, it *could* happen. But they also could gain respect and admiration for you by learning who you are and what you're about, which will help them understand your tenure dossier more clearly. Is it possible that if you cut extraneous projects from your publication pipeline you won't hit the mysterious magical number for promotion? Sure. But it is also possible that you'll feel so liberated and energized that you actually publish more. Worry-fear only presents us with the worst-case scenario while excitement-fear helps us identify new possibilities.

Excitement-fear becomes much more common when we have an abundance mindset. It follows playing big. The fear you felt when I asked you to imagine your publication pipeline filled only with gold-star projects may have been Pachad (worry-fear), but it may have also been Yirah (excitement-fear). To bust out of scarcity mindset and into abundance, we have to recognize worry-fear as just that: fear of the worst-case scenario. Making decisions from this type of fear perpetuates the culture of academia that excludes anyone who is not an able-bodied, cisgender White man.

When some people occasionally experience the worst-case scenario (e.g., cutting a department full of tenured professors), our scarcity mindset is reinforced. The real scarcity of jobs, the mysterious, ever-shifting tenure requirements—all of it plays up the worst-case scenario and feeds a scarcity mindset.

Adopting an abundance mindset means believing deeply that there is *enough* and then taking action as if this is absolutely, 100 percent true. When you believe there is enough time for you to accomplish everything you want to accomplish, you pour time into your most impactful work without fearing that you are missing other opportunities. In other words, you say "no" to requests for your time that may indeed lead to something amazing in order to focus on the work you're doing now, reassured by knowing that there is an abundance of other opportunities that will come your way. When you believe that there are enough resources available to you, you will also choose to say "no" to requests that you know won't lead to opportunities. You don't fear backlash or whispers about not being a team player because you know that even if this job doesn't work out, there are others waiting for you.

When we first begin to break through scarcity into abundance, we feel excitement-fear and often confuse it with worry-fear. The decisions we make will feel daring—even dangerous!

Cutting writing projects that you have already put time and energy into might make your stomach turn. Putting hard boundaries around your time so that you can write and think will mean standing up for yourself and saying "no" to your colleagues—and maybe even your upper administration. It will definitely feel like you are not playing by academia's rules.

And that's because you aren't. You are rewriting the rules, and by doing so, you are remaking academic culture in your image.

When I was in my first year on the tenure track, part of my job was a role called Technology Coordinator. During the interview for this position, the role was painted to be an educational technology role. I thought my work would involve training other faculty members and graduate students to integrate technology into their English language teaching. The reality was that I managed the department's meager technology resources. It was the early 2000s, and we were gravely underresourced, so managing resources meant lending the department's handful of laptops and LCD projectors to faculty who wanted to teach using more than just their chalkboard. It also meant hearing faculty complain about how their printer wasn't working.

In short, it was a nightmare.

But I was well aware of the lack of tenure-track jobs for English PhDs, and on top of that I felt so lucky to have landed this job at my dream institution, the one university in Puerto Rico where both my husband and I could work. But I was miserable.

This can't be what I worked so hard to do! I thought. Worry-fear made me terrified to ask for change. I worried that my colleagues would resent me; I worried that I might be contractually obligated to stay in the role. I thought long and hard about my workload, and I decided that things would be so much better without the Technology Coordinator position. But that was the position for which I'd been hired! I sat on the fence for a year, and after that year, I couldn't take it anymore. I decided to talk to my department chair about it. I was honest and told him that the Technology Coordinator position was not what I expected and asked if I was obligated to continue in the role to keep my job. He quickly said no, and just like that, I was free.

If I had listened to the worry-fear, I would have stayed small. I would have stayed frustrated and overworked in a role I hated. Instead, I faced that fear and believed that I could shape my tenure-track job.

The success of that moment when I took control, when I pushed aside my scarcity mindset and took my career in my own hands, has greatly shaped the way I approach all problems in my career. I made a choice based in abundance. Where scarcity mindset had me thinking I needed to walk on eggshells and keep my head down so that I didn't risk losing my job, a decision based on abundance meant deeply believing that there was more for me—more time, more joy, more status, more impact—and if I couldn't craft that "more" into my current job, abundance mindset let me know that there would be another job for me. Because I was successful at shaping my career in that early moment, I had the confidence and the belief in myself to continue to control my career direction. Instead of scarcity-driven worry-fears driving my decisions ("I can't do X because I might lose my job/make someone angry/not have enough publications/run out of time."), I shifted to a mindset of abundance ("I can make time and space in the job, and if I can't, there are other jobs for me."). With an abundance mindset, I still have fears, but I can recognize them as excitement-fears ("What if I land that grant/what would happen if I just went for it?").

You can fight the twin scarcities ingrained in you by academia. If your internal dialogue often says, "There just aren't enough hours in the day," you can replace that with, "There is enough time for me to accomplish all that I want." If you tell yourself, "I'd better just shut up and try not to lose my job," you can say, "There is room in the world for me in my complete and full form. I don't have to hide or play small."

It's a process. But making decisions from a place of abundance and seeing the results will give you the confidence to continue on an abundant path.

Stepping into abundance can be broken down into a three-step process. For example, maybe you are worried that you won't have enough publications to get tenure.

Step one is to recognize this as a scarcity thought. Ask yourself: What is the origin of this thought? What messages am I getting from my department, my colleagues, even my friends, that are fueling this thought?

Step two is to identify fear-based decisions. Ask yourself: What decisions have I made about publications based on fear? What projects have I said "yes" to that should have been a "no"? What projects am I holding onto thinking that I'll write it someday, when truth be told I never will (and really shouldn't)?

Step three is to take abundant-minded action. Ask yourself: What would I cut from my pipeline if I knew that I had enough publications for tenure? Listen to your fear when you take abundant-minded action. Is it worry-fear or excitement-fear?

So, when you face worry-fear, go through the three steps to reach abundant-minded action:

1. Recognize scarcity thoughts.
2. Identify fear-based decisions.
3. Take abundant-minded action.

Repeat to build momentum.

You can create the career you want. You can create the abundant writing practice you want. It is within your power to kill the twin scarcities for yourself and those around you. This is writing as resistance.

Part 2:

BUILDING A SUSTAINABLE, RELATIONSHIP-BASED WRITING PRACTICE

Chapter 3:
Soaring versus Slogging

A t the end of the first chapter, I argued that developing a thriving writing practice involves a twofold shift: a shift in mindset and a shift in writing as an activity. The conversation about mindset that we started in the second chapter will continue developing as we work through the nuts and bolts of how to create a sustainable, thriving writing practice that leads to publications. In this chapter, I lay out the *relationship-based* how-to of creating a writing practice, i.e., the writing practice that you will create by following the advice in the next few chapters of this book is based on a *positive relationship* with your writing.

I know, academia is a cerebral place. We're not supposed to show up with perceived human limitations, like bodies. And we're especially discouraged from being guided by our feelings. That's why it's revolutionary to focus on how the writing *feels*, rather than on the mechanics of writing or the number of words on the page.

More important than the number of words you write each day, or the amount of time you dedicate to writing during a given week, is your relationship to your writing. You'll develop a writing system that prioritizes your relationship to your writing, and, yes, that includes deliberate action to make the writing feel good.

Unlearning and Relearning Writing

As an adult, you already know that relationships take work. Fostering a great relationship with anything involves intentional actions, reflection, and care. Writing is no different. The problem is, in academia, we've been socialized to have a terrible relationship with our writing. One of my clients once asked me, "Did academia make us forget how to write?"

That question really made me think.

Our relationship to writing develops when we are young. The path is different for everyone, but many of us come to academia with at least some level of "like" for writing and some writing skill. It would be rare to get to a doctoral program without that minimal affinity for writing. Others (and this is where I fit) have had a lifelong love for writing. As a sixth grader I wanted to be a writer. I wrote short stories featuring my classmates and dreamt of becoming a journalist (the only paid writing job my twelve-year-old self could think of). I have always loved to write and considered myself a good writer.

But our childhood reasons for writing—storytelling, expression, etc.—are corrupted by the demands of writing in academia. In academia, writing is about proving that you belong. And as each piece of writing is critiqued and criticized, we can start to believe that we *don't* actually belong. As we journey further into academia, this rhetorical "writing to prove yourself" has higher and higher stakes. The real rhetorical purpose of the dissertation, for example, is not to report findings of original research (that can be done with academic articles); the real rhetorical purpose of the dissertation is to show your committee members that you deserve to become a colleague.

When writing is about proving yourself in a community that is actively trying to weed you out, where is the joy? Where is the intrinsic motivation? The need to express? To communicate? Using writing as a test for membership in the academic community continues throughout academic careers—and only gets worse.

We jump onto the tenure track to become teacher-researchers, though we are often untrained as teachers. This means an extra time burden as we prep for classes and learn to work with students. We are expected to earn tenure mostly by our publications while the majority of our actual day-to-day work involves teaching and service. Writing becomes an invalid assessment of our worth to the academic community, and that feels awful.

The peer review process is also about belonging. I'm not saying that peer review isn't important—it's essential—but all of us have received unhelpful reviews or unexplained desk rejects. When the stakes for publishing are high, that can be devastating. We've all been stopped in our tracks by nasty comments from reviewer number two that made us stop writing for weeks. The lost productivity and time, along with the damage to our relationship with writing, is costly.

If you picked up this book, you are probably ready to unlearn (and relearn) writing. If you no longer like writing or feel like a writer and the academic writing process has become what I like to call "slogging," it is time to unlearn what academia has been teaching you about your relationship with writing.

This unlearning process is completely psychological. It involves mental work and commitment on your part, but it is absolutely worth it, and here's why: if academia has made you forget how to write, or why to write, to the point that you just don't do it anymore, then it's no longer only you with a problem. The world now has a problem because you have a unique perspective on your field that isn't getting out there. It's time to unlearn academia's version of writing. In the free PDF workbook that accompanies this book, I've included step-by-step exercises to help you implement what you read in this chapter. You can get the free workbook by going to https://www.cathymazak.com/workbook.

To go about this "unlearning," I want you to first identify and list your writing stories. These are all the messages that come up when you sit down to think about your writing. For example:

- "I don't know how to write."
- "I have nothing new to say."
- "This is going to get a desk reject."
- "I'm a bad writer."
- "I don't have time to write."

Write it all down, all those voices in your head telling stories about you and your writing. Now take each story and literally flip it on its head. Write exactly the opposite.
- I don't know how to write. → I know how to write.
- I have nothing new to say. → I have new and important things to say.

Next to each new script, write down at least one piece of concrete evidence that supports your new positive statement. For example, for "I know how to write," you might say, "One of my committee members commented that she was moved by parts of my dissertation."

It doesn't matter how small or insignificant you perceive the evidence to be. What matters is that it is true and supports your new script.

Now each time one of those old, negative stories comes into your head, you need to repeat your new story. We have thousands of thoughts per day. Changing our default thoughts takes diligence. Try writing your new stories on paper and hanging them on the wall or setting an alarm on your phone and reading your new stories out loud to yourself several times per day. When your old stories come back, try shooing them away with a phrase like "not help-ful." If you have to say it out loud, do it!

Do whatever it takes to relearn your relationship with writing. If you were a writer as a kid, remember the rea-sons you wrote then. You had a story to tell, a message to communicate, something to say! Connect with that kiddo and honor her and her human need to communicate. You can find her again—and believe that she has something important to say.

Soaring versus Slogging

As you work to unlearn the negative messages you tell yourself about your writing and who you are as a writer, you'll need to deliberately take actions to foster a positive relationship with writing.

I'm going to say something that probably no one has ever told you.

Writing should feel good.

You've been conditioned through the culture of aca-demia to revel in struggle. If you don't feel overworked, have deadlines coming up too fast, and fall behind in grad-ing, you are obviously doing it wrong. I'm here to tell you that academia doesn't have to feel like you are running on a treadmill set two clicks too fast. Your work doesn't have to feel like a struggle.

In fact, if you can make writing feel good, making the rest of your academic life feel good is well within your reach.

What does it mean for writing to feel good? Think back to writing sessions in your past. Sometimes we sit down to write, and the words just flow out. Other times we write nine words and delete five, write another six and delete four. In those sessions, writing feels like slogging! I specifically remember working on an abstract for a conference presentation at 4:00 in the afternoon. The abstract was for a local conference, and I just wanted to write those two hundred words before picking up my daughter at daycare by 5 p.m. so that I could check it off my list. I painfully toiled for forty-five minutes only to produce about fifty words.

I finally just gave up and headed to my car flustered, feeling like a failure. The next morning, I decided to tackle the abstract first thing. I banged out those two hundred words in half an hour! Clear ideas were flowing out of my brain and through my fingers with complete and utter ease.

So, what was the difference between the writing session that felt like slogging and the one that felt like soaring? And more importantly, how can we manufacture soaring and avoid slogging? That is the central question that underlies the writing system you will build following the advice in this chapter.

Why Writing Every Day Backfires

Standard writing advice says in answer to the question *"How can I write more?"*: *"Do it."* Do it every day. Don't miss a day. Hit a word count. Put accountability systems in place so that you continue to write.

Every. Single. Day.

The idea is that the thing keeping you from writing is your fear of putting words on the page, so you get over this fear by just putting words on the page continually, even if it means extreme editing later. This line of thought follows that if you work out your writing muscle every day, you will eventually get over your fear of writing and you will have strengthened your writing muscle enough to flex it whenever you need to.

But the "write every day" advice doesn't consider slogging and soaring. It isn't honoring your relationship with your writing or paying attention to how it feels. Because of this, "write every day" advice reinforces the belief that your academic work must include suffering.

Write, even if it feels like slogging.

Write, even if you hate every minute of it.

Just as I've argued that womxn and nonbinary people need to reject the culture of overwork that is so glorified within the racist patriarchy of academia, we also need to reject the idea that suffering is part of the work. If you've tried to write every day and it hasn't worked, you're not alone. This method has never worked for me for two main reasons.

1. You slip and feel guilty.

If your goal is writing every day, what happens when you don't? What happens when your kid gets a fever, your department chair throws you a fire to put out, or you wake up sick and tired? You miss a day. And then the worst: you feel guilty.

Guilt is the biggest obstacle to writing and publishing more.

Have you ever had a half-done article sitting on your computer? You know that you need to finish it, but you can never find the time. Every time you remember it, you get a wave of guilt. Or have you ever had a really tough semester, when you know you've taken on too much, so you haven't been keeping up with your writing? Guilt again.

Guilt stomps down writing spark. It inhibits creativity. It pretty much guarantees that you will feel awful once you sit down to start writing again. Trying to write every day just sets you up for more guilt when you inevitably (and understandably) can't do it. Instead, you need a writing system that deliberately sets you up for success. That in its very essence is designed to make you feel happy about your writing, which in turn creates a positive feedback loop between you and your writing: you write, you feel good, you write, you feel good. Every time. And that brings me to problem number two with trying to write every day.

2. Not all writing sessions are created equal.

Remember soaring versus slogging? Sometimes you sit down, and the words just flow out of you. When you go back to read it, you think, "I'm amazing!" Other times, you sit down to write just one paragraph and end up writing five words and deleting three for an hour so that by the end of your writing session you only have a sentence or two. And after all that slogging you thought, "What the heck is wrong with me?"

Not all writing sessions are created equal.

You need to set yourself up to write with that soaring feeling and deliberately avoid writing when it's a slogging feeling. If your writing system is "write every day," you might be hitting your flow, but you also might not. And the problem is that when you don't hit those flow times but sit down and just try to bang out a certain number of words anyway because that is what your system requires, then you can create a negative feedback loop between you and your writing: you write, you feel bad, you write, you feel bad. Then you'll stop. Or you'll hate writing. That's how the "write every day" model blows up in your face.

The "write every day" philosophy rests on the idea that you need to get a certain number of words on the page and then severely edit. It doesn't matter if you write one thousand crappy words; somewhere in there are two or three hundred brilliant words. You just need to write a lot and edit down. But if one of your obstacles to writing more is lack of time, you don't have time to write one thousand words to get two hundred.

And it's not *just* a lack of time. Writing is so much about how we *feel*. And writing one thousand words to get two hundred can feel icky. Worse, doing something every day is sometimes just impossible. If we set that unreasonable expectation for ourselves, then we can set ourselves up for feeling like failures when we can't meet it. And nothing shuts down writing faster than feeling like a failure—especially a guilty failure.

Writing Relationship Renewal

Instead of relying on "write every day" to move the needle, you need a system that creates a positive feedback loop between you and your writing. This is an intentionally designed system with various parts, but at its essence is one core idea.

Write during your best, most driven, highest-energy times (what I'm going to call your "Soaring State"). Do not write at other times (what I'm going to call your "Slogging State").

The goal of this writing system is to improve your relationship with your writing so much that every writing session is a Soaring Session and you end up excited when you sit down to write.

When you combine this improved writing relationship with reframing your career to put writing at the center, your writing will not only be supporting your career advancement (i.e., getting a promotion) but it will also be defining who you are as a scholar and driving your career in the direction that you want it to go—on your terms. Writing will no longer feel like slogging, the thing that falls to the bottom of the list, or the guilt-inducing, ever-present worry in your head. And once that shift occurs, you will be in a powerful position to use your writing to define your career.

Finding Your "Soaring State"

We've already talked about the difference between writing sessions when the words just pour out of you and writing sessions when it feels heavy to tap the keys: the Soaring Session versus the Slogging Session.

The difference between soaring and slogging is in energy and drive. When you're soaring, you are supported by invisible energy, moving forward steadily, with a high-level vision of where you want to go. When you're slogging, you're in the weeds, barely putting one metaphorical foot in front of the other.

To create a positive relationship with your writing, you need to *create* the drive and energy that powers the Soaring Session and purposefully avoid the Slogging Session.

You are most likely to create a Soaring Session during your best, most easeful, highest-energy time of day, which I call your "Soaring State." In your Soaring State, you are a bird with outstretched wings, moved forward and upward by invisible energy. A soaring bird does not flap its wings, struggling against the wind. A soaring bird is easily taking advantage of its power and leveraging energy. During your Soaring State, tasks that can take forever at other times of day come easily to you. The difference between me struggling to write a short abstract at 4 p.m. and the abstract practically writing itself the next morning came from writing during my Slogging State versus writing during my

Soaring State. Your Soaring State is found in the time of day when your writing just flows.

Once you learn to identify your Soaring State, you can make big strides in your writing by writing just two to three hours a week during that time. You'll potentially make far more progress than by following the "write every day" model.

In fact, when you learn how to harness your Soaring State, knowing when *not* to write is just as important as knowing when to write.

I first became aware of my Soaring State when I worked as a technical writer for a software company in Ann Arbor, Michigan right after graduating with my bachelor's degree in English from Indiana University Bloomington. Working as a technical writer was pure cubicle life, completely nine-to-five. Frankly, I hated it. I would go to work, sit down, and tear through things on my list until about 11:30 a.m. Then my ability to get stuff done slowed down, and work felt like wading through molasses. Afternoons were torture. I could get done in three morning hours what it took other people eight or more hours to do, and I sat bored in a cubicle for the rest of the time I had to be there. Part of my desire to go to grad school came from wanting to bust out of that nine-to-five cubicle life (ironically, after getting on the tenure track, I'd be doing everything I could to fit my work back into nine-to-five, but more on that later). I recognized in my first cubicle job that I could take on the world between 8:00 and 11:00 a.m., but I didn't learn how to use that to my advantage until much later.

One of the most important things that you can do to successfully write and publish more is to know thyself. You need to know the writing methods that work for you, you need to intimately know your publication pipeline, and you need to know how long it takes you to do certain writing-related tasks (more on these in coming chapters). And the only way to learn these things about yourself is through reflection, which is exactly the tool you'll use.

To find your Soaring State, you'll need to be very reflective for three to five days. You'll do this by keeping a Soaring State journal. In the free PDF workbook I created for you, you'll find a downloadable Soaring State journal that supports the reflective process I'm about to teach you. You can go get it at https://www.cathymazak.com/workbook. To create this journal yourself, simply make a table with days across the top and your waking hours listed underneath. It will look like this:

Monday	Tuesday	Wednesday
6:00 a.m.	6:00 a.m.	6:00 a.m.
7:00 a.m.	7:00 a.m.	7:00 a.m.
8:00 a.m.	8:00 a.m.	8:00 a.m.

(Keep going; you get it.)

Now, you might already know that you are a morning person or a night owl, but take the time to do this exercise to pinpoint your specific best (and worst) times for writing. You probably have an absolute best time and a second-best time, along with times when you absolutely should avoid trying to write. By identifying these times and understanding that you would just be wasting time to try to write during your worst times, you get rid of guilt and let go of the idea that you should be writing twenty-four seven. This is key to renewing your relationship with writing.

You're going to keep this journal for three to five days. You can choose working days to focus on, but Soaring State holds on weekends as well. As you move through your day, you're going to note in your journal during all the hours when you are awake. About every hour, pull out your journal and reflect on how you're feeling. Then mark that hour with a color from the following key:

- Green: the most energy, inspiration, and drive
- Blue: still pretty energized but need to take more breaks to sustain momentum
- Orange: easily distracted, bored, tired, procrastinating
- Red: complete exhaustion; there's no way you're getting anything done

After three to five days, you'll see your patterns of energy, and your Soaring State time will be quite obvious. Once you're done, write down your Soaring State (green and blue) and your Slogging State (orange and red) times.

Once you've identified your Soaring State, you need to mark it on your calendar. When planning writing sessions during your Soaring State, don't try to block off more than two hours at a time, even if you feel like you have more than two green Soaring State hours in the day. It is not realistic to write for more than a solid two hours every day unless you are on a writing retreat. What you're looking to do is create a consistent routine, and few of us have more than two hours per day to write. If you do, that's great! But most of us are balancing teaching, meetings, and our personal lives, so two hours is good enough. It's actually more than good enough, because if you consistently use the two most inspirational hours of your day for writing, you'll be far more productive than if you block five hours every once in a while.

If you can't do two hours in a row, that's fine. Try to do one hour during your Soaring State and another hour during your blue second-best time. If you can only do one hour or thirty minutes, that's fine too. The important thing is being realistic and consistent. Your task, then, is to pull out your calendar and begin your Soaring State journey with a small commitment: one to two hours of writing per day once or twice a week during your Soaring State. Mark this on your calendar as a date with your writing and honor it as an appointment.

You may be thinking that one to four hours a week of writing is not nearly enough for everything that you have to get done. This belief is rooted in the way you have successfully written big projects before. You've maybe written five hundred words a day and then spent tons of time editing those five hundred slogging words. Or maybe you've blocked a whole day or weekend for writing and "binged." These methods may have gotten you results in the short term, but they are unsustainable in the long term. Remember, during your Soaring State, you can write a lot more words effectively than when you employ "write every day" or binge writing, so shorter amounts of time produce more usable writing. Also remember that you are aiming to build a process that improves your relationship with writing. You need to start slow, gain confidence, and work your way up to more hours (if you can sustainably do so).

Trust me, one to two hours once or twice a week is going to be enough, and soon you will see the results it has in actual words on the page. Eventually you might choose to work up to one to two hours three to five times a week as an absolute maximum, but I want you to see the power of one to two hours once or twice a week first.

Now that you've blocked your precious one to two hours once or twice a week during your Soaring State, you need to get real. Many people find that they are routinely doing nonwriting tasks during their Soaring State. For example, my Soaring State is 8:00 a.m. to around 11:00 a.m. During a typical semester, I would be getting my kids ready and doing school drop-off during that time, and I probably wouldn't land at my desk until 8:30 a.m. with just enough time to catch my breath for a 9 a.m. class. When I had time in my schedule to write, it would usually land squarely in my Slogging State.

The solution is to change your schedule.

Yes, you read that right.

Writing is not only the best way to control your scholarly development but you as a womxn or nonbinary person prioritizing your writing is an act of resistance that disrupts the racist, ableist patriarchy. If academic culture is going to change, it requires you as an individual to take action toward changing it. One key way to do this is to prioritize writing in your schedule.

You will most certainly face a myriad of challenges when it comes to altering your schedule to fit your writing times instead of altering your writing times to fit your schedule (which is what most people do). You might be reading this book mid-semester with classes already in full swing during your Soaring State, you may be in a department in which you have little agency around your schedule, or you might have found that your Soaring State is smack in the middle of something like school pick-up or drop-off. I invite you to release the constraints you have built in your head about all the reasons you can't block your Soaring State off for writing one to two hours one to two times per week. When we think about implementing advice or trying something new, our lizard brain often recoils screaming, "Not safe! Not for me!" It's time to break through those initial "never could I ever" thoughts and think creatively.

Create a three-column table with as many rows as you need (I created this for you in the free downloadable workbook, which you can find at https://cathymazak.com/workbook.)

In column one, list all the things standing in the way of you blocking your Soaring State in your calendar for writing one to two hours one to two times per week. For example, "My child's school drop-off time falls during my Soaring State."

In column two, write your "never could I ever" statements. For each reason you listed in column one, rewrite it in the form of "never could I ever." To continue with the above example, you'd write, "Never could I ever NOT drop off my child at school."

In column three, list all the alternatives that would make the "never could I ever" statement false. Word them as "I could" statements. For our example, "I could ask my partner to drop off the kids twice a week. My kids could take the bus. I could pay a service to drop off my kids. I could ask a friend to drop off the kids twice a week." List as many "I could" statements as possible. Please note, these are not "I would," "I will," or "I can" statements. You are just making a list of humanly possible statements. You are not committing to any of them yet.

This "never could I ever" exercise was designed to stir the pot, to get you thinking. What became possible that once seemed impossible? When you allowed your brain to run with possibilities, did you find some that you could try?

Removing the obstacles to prioritizing your writing is *work*. It is a completely new way of thinking about your schedule. Prioritizing your writing is a version of prioritizing yourself, and we are socialized to prioritize everybody else first. But this shift to using your very best energy to write, and then creating your schedule around that, is the first step in centering your writing in your career, which has major payoffs for you and your happiness.

Implementing changes to liberate your Soaring State for writing may take time. For example, if you are teaching during your Soaring State, it may take months or even years to adjust your teaching schedule. Take it slow and work on making the changes that you can easily make first. If you find that you are often checking your email during your Soaring State, you can easily stop this practice right now. Make those easy schedule changes first, and work on the harder schedule adjustments over time.

Keeping Appointments with Your Writing

It's easy to understand the importance of writing and the mechanics of blocking sessions during your Soaring State, but it's harder to honor those sessions. Writing sessions are often the first appointments to get scheduled over. If you've come this far in the chapter and this sounds familiar, it's time for some real talk.

One of the greatest lessons in parenting is learning how it's suddenly easy to bump seemingly unbumpable tasks from your schedule when something happens to your child. If your child is ill and needs to go to the doctor, you will immediately clear your schedule to make that happen. When I first started teaching, I would accept any class time, even if it was inconvenient or during my Soaring State. But once I was in charge of the kids' morning drop-off, I drew a hard line in the sand that I could no longer teach at 8 a.m. Done. No early morning classes.

It is easy to completely rearrange our lives and our schedules for our children or other "outside" responsibilities. It's much harder to rearrange our schedules for *ourselves*. But it is both possible to do so and necessary.

This is the hard truth of academia: no one will save you. You have to save yourself. If your institution's leadership had their way, you would be teaching five courses with research and external funding expectations, plus tons of service. That is the reality of this job.

And let's be clear, academia is just that: a job. The idea that we should be willing to do our jobs twenty-four seven is toxic. To avoid burnout, you need to put up some firm boundaries—real fast. One of those boundaries needs to be around your writing time.

It's hard to look your colleagues in the eye and tell them, "No, I can't meet then because it's my writing time." Or to ask your partner to pick up the kids because you're writing. Women in particular are socialized against this type of boundary-setting, and we think we will appear selfish or rude by setting those boundaries. But let me describe the alternative to you. If you are not in a tenure-track job, not honoring your writing time means not getting a tenure-track job. If you are pretenure and do not write, you will lose your job. If you are post-tenure, you will sit in associate professor purgatory, like so many who never make it to full professor.

Am I being a bit dramatic? Okay, here's a less dramatic version of what will happen if you don't honor your writing time: you will constantly feel guilty and overwhelmed, like you have too much on your plate to do what you *really* want to do, and that will lead to burnout. People throw the term "burnout" around as a synonym for exhaustion, but it's more serious than that. If you burn out, you will need to disappear from your job for several weeks, possibly in the middle of the semester. I know because this has happened to me. It is not pretty, and it's not fun. This "I'll keep going and going and I won't make time for what I really want" mentality has the opposite effect than you intend. Not honoring your writing time will catch up with you, and it will backfire badly.

To close this section about keeping appointments with your writing, I want to emphasize something I tell clients who tend to make a plan and then not stick to it.

Not being able to stick to your plans
is a matter of self-trust.

Womxn in particular are socialized to not trust themselves. Womxn were not trusted, for example, to have their own bank accounts without a male cosigner until the late 1970s. Womxn are not trusted to describe their own pain to a doctor or even to listen to their own bodies during childbirth. A womxn who trusts herself is a dangerous person. So, if you find yourself making plans and not sticking to them, you are operating exactly as the patriarchy has conditioned you to operate.

Full disclosure: I am someone who struggles to follow her own plans! I love the planning part of any project—the mapping out, figuring out the order of things, breaking the project down, getting the pieces onto my calendar.

Sticking to that plan is harder. I veer off with the feeble excuse, "I just don't feel like doing it that way today."

To overcome this self-doubt disguised as whim, I think, "Trust your past self."

I remind myself that my planning self of a few days or weeks ago knew exactly what she was doing. "Stick to the plan" is written on a post-it note stuck to my computer because I know my planning self had my present self's best interests at heart. And then I stick to the plan.

The Importance of *Not* Writing

All this talk about when to write mandates a conversation about when *not* to write. The flip side of honoring your Soaring State (your green and blue times) is to honor your Slogging State, (your orange and red times). Equally important as deciding when *to* write is deciding (and honoring) when *not* to write.

When you decide not to write during your Slogging State, you are released from feeling guilty when you're not writing because it is actually counterproductive to write during your Slogging State. Writing during your Soaring State cultivates flow and momentum. Deliberately avoiding writing at other times eliminates feeling like you should be writing twenty-four seven.

The concept of soaring versus slogging works very well for those who struggle with guilt about writing because part of the system's design is to schedule writing for specific times and to NOT schedule writing at other times. This gives you permission to not be writing all the time.

It's also good for people who feel overwhelmed by writing because it breaks up writing into smaller time slots and makes it a regular habit. Honoring your Soaring State also works well if you feel like you need a "spark" to write, because it places writing in your most energetic window of the day—when you are most likely to feel "spark." It also helps establish, or reestablish, lost momentum because it works with your energy, not against it.

Renewing your relationship with your writing is dependent on honoring both your Soaring State AND your Slogging State. Deciding when to write and when not to write are two sides of the same coin. You have my permission to write only during your Soaring State and to let all the other times go.

Troubleshooting the Soaring State

In teaching this method to hundreds of clients over the years, some have faced bumps on the road to finding and using their Soaring State. In this section, I'll dig into these roadblocks and offer possible solutions, but if you haven't tried the Soaring State method to see how it works for you, you can skip this part and come back if and when you encounter one of these problems (In other words, don't let the possibility of these problems stop you from trying Soaring Sessions!).

What if I can't hit the perfect moment for writing? Although you will be more productive if you listen to your daily energy cycles and write during your Soaring State, sometimes it's just not possible. The key is not to use that as an excuse. Can't hit your best time? Schedule during your second-best time. Can't block more than one Soaring State hour per week? Just start with one hour.

What if I never feel the energy and drive you're describing, so I can't identify my Soaring State? This is a problem for some people with chronic illnesses, who are pregnant or breastfeeding, and who are exhausted by parenting or other caretaking roles, but frankly this inability to find your Soaring State can happen to anyone for many different reasons. If you're having trouble feeling the Soaring State, the first solution is to try getting some serious rest. As a mom of three, I know that this is not always possible, but what you really need is a restorative week off. If you can't get that rest, or rest just won't solve your problem (as is the case with some types of chronic conditions), then try cowriting.

Cowriting simply means writing at the same time and in the same place (virtual or physical) as someone else. Not only does cowriting help you keep a date with your writing (since you also must keep a date with another person) but it also helps you stay focused and on task. In this sense, cowriting can help create the Soaring State. You feel energy and drive being uplifted by others who are writing at the same time as you. In my programs, I run cowriting sessions with academics around the world via Zoom. You could find a friend and meet at the library to cowrite together.

I used to know my Soaring State, but it seems to have shifted. There is a saying in business: "What got you here won't get you there." This is true in writing as well. The strategies you've been using to get writing done change with every major life event, including switching jobs, moving, having a child, getting promoted, falling ill, etc. Every major thing that happens in your life is a reason to reevaluate your writing system—and your Soaring State. Many womxn and nonbinary people struggle in their first year on the tenure track because they are trying to write using the same practices that they developed as graduate students when the demands of the tenure track are vastly different from the demands of graduate school. Post-tenure faculty describe the same shift after they are awarded tenure: the strategies they were previously using to write seem to no longer work in this new phase of their career.

This is totally normal. When we learn to expect the shift instead of thinking there is something wrong with us, we can better solve the problem of a shifting Soaring State.

If you feel like your Soaring State is different or has "stopped working," reflect on whether any major changes have occurred in both your professional and personal life. Acknowledge those and then redo the Finding Your Soaring State exercise. You may find that your Soaring State has simply shifted, and now you must go through the work of freeing and protecting that new time.

I repeat, this is totally normal!

In this chapter, you learned how to use your best, most energetic times of day (your Soaring State) for writing and why to avoid your Slogging State. The purpose of this is to create writing sessions that are Soaring Sessions, during which you feel supported by invisible energy as you write. This system for writing prioritizes your relationship with your writing, creating positive feedback loops as you have enjoyable encounters with your writing again and again.

In the next chapter, we'll zoom out and look at how writing can become the driving force behind your entire career.

Chapter 4:

Writing at the Center

When you plan for the week, the month, or the year, what goes onto your calendar first? For most academics, the answer is teaching. Then regular department and faculty meetings are sketched in. At that point, if you have a lab, you might find your lab meeting times. You'll block your required number of office hours and the times you'll set aside to meet with graduate students. If you like planning, you might even map in major conference and grant deadlines.

But when does writing fit into your schedule? Does it go onto your calendar fifth? Tenth? Does it go on your calendar at all?

> The great irony of academic culture is that
> while publications are revered, writing time
> is relegated to the periphery of our calendars.

We fit writing in on nights and weekends, or we wake up early to get in some writing before the day "truly starts." We wait for big blocks of time to write that never come or block off Friday afternoons to write only to collapse at the end of the week. Writing falls to the bottom of the list. It lives on the edges.

Everything is more urgent than writing. Because there are rarely deadlines for submitting journal articles and book proposals, the decision to put off writing in favor of grading, class prep, or meeting with that colleague who keeps begging for your time seems reasonable. Writing can wait. Students and colleagues cannot.

At least, that's what it feels like.

But when you repeatedly choose the urgent over the important, you're constantly putting out fires. More directly, you're choosing *others* over *yourself*, which is exactly what the patriarchy expects womxn and nonbinary people to do over and over again until they burn out.

I had my third (and final!) baby in 2016. It was my third maternity leave, and I was already a full professor. I knew from my experience with my previous two children that motherhood in those early months was physically and mentally taxing. I knew I wouldn't be sleeping well. My body would need time to heal. I knew that I didn't want to look at even one measly work email during those precious first months with my last baby. So, I designed a complete disconnect for myself during maternity—and I say "designed" because it was absolutely deliberate. I cleared my publication pipeline before my due date, didn't take on new projects or students during my pregnancy, and was able to successfully dial down work to nothing and enjoy my time with baby.

When I came back, the publications I had cleared from my pipeline that were submitted in their final or near-final states during the last months of my pregnancy were born into the world. It just so happened that these included two edited volumes and an article in a top-tier journal. One day as I was walking down the hall, a senior colleague in my department stopped me. "Congratulations on your book!" she said, genuinely excited for me. "Did you write it during maternity leave?"

The comment stopped me dead in my tracks. Since I was still in the throes of first-year baby care—including getting woken up multiple times a night—my first reaction was to wonder how someone who was also a mother could possibly think that writing a book with an infant was even possible.

But the truly shocking thing is what this comment says about writing being relegated to the edges of our time. My colleague couldn't imagine how I'd been able to write a book without taking leave (no matter that the purpose of the leave was to have a baby, not write a book). Is writing so peripheral that you have to literally leave your job to make it happen? Isn't *writing* the job?

I admit that writing a book with a 4-4 load wasn't easy, but I designed my career to make it happen. I put writing at the center of my career, and writing was the driving force.

If writing is important—and it *is*—it cannot be on the edges. It must sit firmly at the center with everything else supporting it. The idea that academic womxn and nonbinary people should organize their time around their writing, rather than around their teaching or meeting schedule, is revolutionary. It flies in the face of expectations to put others first. But it also aligns with the way we are evaluated as academics, with publications as a weighty factor. If we are to continue being evaluated on our publications, we must start to treat writing as *the* central activity of our careers.

Although, I will say, I'm not actually in favor of publication-heavy evaluation criteria. So let me put it another way. You have a unique, once-only-on-earth message to get out into the world. If you've picked up this book, you know that writing is an important way to get that message out there. Maybe you want to be louder in that message. So, if you're ready for a revolutionary way to organize your career, let's explore organizing your career around writing.

Is Writing on the Periphery or in the Center?

Writing can feel so important that you may think, "Of course writing is central for me!" But how you think about writing, or what you believe about its role in your career right now, might not be supported by the actions you're taking. Here are five clues that writing is on the periphery for you.

Clue #1: You wake up early, stay up late, or work weekends to write.

As a mom of three kids who were all horrible sleepers, the popular suggestion that I should simply wake up before my kids to write or write after they went to bed truthfully just made me angry. My son woke up between 4 and 4:30 a.m. *for the day* from the time he was a toddler through early elementary school. My daughter required me to lie by her side until she fell asleep each night, which of course meant that I usually fell asleep right along with her. By the time I got to bedtime, I was too exhausted to peel myself out of her bed and sit down to write—or even to brush my teeth!

But my maternal exhaustion is not the point. The point is that suggesting people, especially womxn, use their personal time—or worse, *their sleeping hours*—to do the most important activity of their careers, the activity on which they will be evaluated for promotion, for getting a job and keeping a job, is seriously screwed up. It is saying that writing is not actually important. If it were important, it would fit into their core working hours.

Again, academia reveres publications, but not the writing it takes to get them done. Try telling a CFO they should wake up early to review profit and loss statements before they go to the office when reviewing profit and loss statements is the most important activity of their job. It doesn't make any sense.

Some people will insist that they write on the weekends because it is the only time when they can have relatively clear blocks of hours without interruption. If you need relatively clear blocks of hours without interruption to write, and you are not getting that during your work-week, writing is on the periphery of your career, not at the center. If you try creating Soaring Sessions for yourself, which don't require big blocks of time, and you still long for days or half-days without interruption, then you will create them if writing is important (I'll talk about how later in this chapter). Hear this tough love clearly: if writing is only happening on nights and weekends, then it is on the periphery of your career.

Clue #2: Your work schedule is designed around your teaching schedule.

Like many universities, mine held fifty-minute classes on Mondays, Wednesdays, and Fridays and ninety-minute classes on Tuesdays and Thursdays. We also had a "universal hour" on Tuesdays and Thursdays from 10:30 a.m. to 12:00 p.m. when no classes could be scheduled. Students used this time for clubs and student groups, and professors used this time for meetings. Not surprisingly, since we had this preordained block when everyone was supposed to be "free," there were *a lot* of meetings. Every Tuesday and Thursday at 10:30 a.m., I had a committee meeting, and it was the same for everyone in the department. That made Tuesday and Thursday teaching schedules extra coveted because you had to come to campus anyway, so you might as well smush everything onto Tuesdays and Thursdays and then have Mondays, Wednesdays, and Fridays open to schedule as you wish.

As a new professor, I was scheduled to teach Mondays, Wednesdays, and Fridays in the early morning. I didn't mind because I liked the rhythm of fifty-minute classes, and I didn't feel like I could complain too much. But when I realized that my Soaring State was first thing in the morning, I had to make a change. By the time I got to campus on Tuesdays and Thursdays after dropping off my kids, I only had about an hour each day of Soaring State. That was okay at first, but then I was ready for more, and I started to rearrange my teaching schedule around my writing time.

If you resist your Soaring State because it lands squarely in the hours you always teach, writing is not at the center. If you are working as an adjunct with little control over your schedule, piecing together a salary by teaching at more than one university and can't build your schedule around writing, the point still stands. Writing is not at the center. The system is set up for this to be so, putting you forever on a teaching treadmill where writing gets pushed to the edges and you stay stuck.

How academics in different positions of privilege and power go about restructuring their teaching time around their writing will necessarily differ. It may be a years-long process as you negotiate small changes that bring you closer and closer to honoring your Soaring State by teaching at other times. But no matter your situation, teaching during your writing time is still a symptom that writing is at the periphery for you.

Clue #3: Your course content centers the generic department syllabus and not your work.

Were you hired to teach a certain course, but that course is no longer your area of research focus? So many of the academic womxn and nonbinary people I coach feel burdened by courses that they've outgrown, or that they never loved in the first place, but feel obligated to keep teaching because they are perceived as the only person in their department who can. Or maybe you've been handed a generic department syllabus and you've felt obligated to teach that course content the same way others have because that's just the way it's done at your university.

With writing at the center of your career, your teaching supports your writing. When I first began my tenure-track work, I taught a horribly named course: pre-basic English. As an incoming first-year student at one of Puerto Rico's most prestigious universities having experienced mandatory English as a subject in school since kindergarten, to be placed in a class that was *lower than* basic English was cruel and disheartening.

But I loved teaching those students. I spent most of my energy trying to show them that they already knew so much more than the system acknowledged. The rest of the time, though, I had to teach them how to correctly form the verb "to be," because that's what the curriculum mandated.

During this time, I began to develop a line of research around what was then the newly named phenomenon *translanguaging*. I would read about code-switching, bilingual learning, and sociocultural approaches to language teaching, and then I would walk into that overpacked classroom—the one with no air conditioning, a couple of squeaking ceiling fans, and slatted windows that students propped open with empty Coke cans because the crank mechanisms no longer worked. I couldn't in good faith keep teaching "pre-basic" English while developing a line of research about translanguaging. So, a talented master's student and I designed a study that showed that there was no difference in the performance of students who took "pre-basic" English before basic English, and after a lot of departmental fighting, the university got rid of the class.

After throwing off the burden of "pre-basic" English, I looked for courses to teach where I could dig into translanguaging with my students. I took on the linguistics senior seminar, and everyone did translanguaging projects. I took on the sociolinguistics graduate course, and we studied how translanguaging grew out of traditional sociolinguistics.

I turned every syllabus towards translanguaging, and that dissonance I felt when I walked into the "pre-basic" English classroom melted away. My teaching became about my research, and I stopped feeling pulled in a thousand directions. What I was writing about was also what I was teaching about, so it made perfect sense to build my days around writing and let my teaching support that.

Clue #4: You can't keep a date with your writing.

It's good advice to put writing on your calendar as if it's an appointment—but it's useless if you can't keep that date. Think about other things you put on your calendar and keep as appointments—doctor's appointments, for example. If a colleague came to you and asked if you could meet to discuss curriculum changes when you had a doctor's appointment on your calendar, would you cancel it to meet with your colleague? Or let's say you had a meeting with a graduate student to go over feedback on their thesis. Would you move that appointment aside for your colleague?

Yet, you would cancel a writing appointment.

Why? Because the appointment is with yourself?

Going back to my example, your health is important, and so is the doctor's time. Maybe the appointment was with a specialist, so you made it months ago. These are all good reasons not to cancel. Your student depends on you to move forward with their thesis. They took time to prepare for the meeting and are eager to learn from you—also good reasons not to cancel.

If writing is at the center—if you make it as important as you know it is for your career and for getting your voice into the world—you can't cancel appointments with your writing. If you're doing that, writing is on the periphery.

Clue #5: You don't have your pipeline visibly mapped out.

A publication pipeline is a metaphor, but that doesn't mean it shouldn't have a concrete representation somewhere. A pipeline is an ordered list of all the publications you have "in play," from those that are just writing ideas to those you've revised and resubmitted. If you're holding on to all of that in your head, then writing is on the periphery. You can use something as simple as sticky notes on a wall or as fancy as a Trello board, but your pipeline needs to be visible somewhere that you check often.

Just don't write it on a white board in your office where cleaning staff can erase it, like one of my clients did. She opened her office one day to find her meticulously crafted whiteboard pipeline completely cleaned away!

If your writing is at the center, then you have your finger on the pulse of all your "in play" writing projects and a place to park ideas for new projects.

Rebellious Reflections

1. What are some clues that writing is at the periphery for you? Which of these five clues resonates?

2. Look at your calendar. What is at the center for you right now? What always takes precedence? What would you cancel appointments for?

3. What is one change that you can implement to make writing more central?

Putting writing at the center of your career means making choices that prioritize not only your writing time but also the spaciousness, calm, and time to think that supports writing. Writing drives your decision-making. By using writing as a guiding force, the often disparate activities of academic work line up. Instead of feeling pulled in a thousand directions by research, teaching, and service (and all the subcategories of these), one organizing force—

your writing—drives everything. The result is that your career feels like it's about *one thing*, instead of many things competing for your attention.

How many times have you said to yourself, "If I wasn't so busy, I'd have time to think!" Putting writing at the center allows for spaciousness and calm to enter and gives you a centrality of purpose that allows for the kind of thinking so many academics seek.

Writing Drives Decisions about Time

Your writing should drive your decisions about time. This begins with building your schedule. Instead of mapping in meetings and teaching time first, then fitting writing around those "appointments," writing goes on your calendar first, and everything else must bend to fit.

If you're using Soaring Sessions, that means your Soaring State times or your cowriting times are blocked as appointments on your calendar. If you insist on needing big blocks of time to write, then you must find those blocks and protect them *first*. Granted, this advice assumes a certain amount of autonomy around your schedule that you may not feel you have. Know that this is a process. It may take you multiple semesters of petitioning to get your course schedule changed to better support your writing time, but the fight is worth it. It will definitely take you multiple semesters of enforcing and reinforcing boundaries with colleagues to change the way you schedule meetings. But again, it is worth it.

> For writing to alter your career, it needs to be the priority on your calendar.

Writing cannot be left to fit into the edges of your time. That means your writing time should be scheduled during your working hours, not on nights and weekends. Even more difficult to implement is *not working on nights and weekends at all.* If you move writing into the central time of your calendar just to push everything else onto nights and weekends, you will burn out. The idea that academics can and should work sixty-, seventy-, or eighty-hour weeks so that their hourly rate ends up being less than minimum wage is fast capitalism at its best. You absolutely need space and time to restore yourself. You need space and time to *think*, which is your job! If you are not getting that, you are not positioned to do the writing that you need to do to sustain your career.

> Let me say that again: If you are not taking the space and time you need to restore yourself, you are not positioned to do the writing that you need to do to sustain your career.

By continuing to overwork, put in long hours, and exhaust yourself, you are quieting your voice. You are working under conditions that impair your ability to make the contribution you want to make to your field, and you are robbing yourself of the opportunity to have the career and life you want. The injustice of adjuncting and contingency is voices being silenced by unsustainable working conditions, and the tragedy of overwork is that it silences those who bear its burden, which is inequitably carried by womxn, especially womxn of color. If you are being crushed by the weight of your career, you feel academia pushing you out.

But what to do? Can you simply stop working nights and weekends? Just stop doing it all? Don't grade those papers? Don't write those exams? The answer to that depends a lot on the type of academic position that you are in. It's not as simple as "if you're an adjunct you can't" and "if you're a full professor you can." *Everyone* should reexamine their boundaries and take stock of what they are doing based on fear or what once might have been true. If you're a full professor working nights and weekends because the work doesn't fit into the week, are you making decisions based on the fear of not getting tenure when that hurdle is actually in your past? We become conditioned in our decision-making just like in everything else. To push back against the system that wants you to keep working eighty-hour weeks, you need to examine your own decision-making and determine what you can control. Then you must work to control what you can.

When work floods over into nights and weekends, we sometimes think, *How did I get here?* That thought can lead to judgment and self-blame. You got here through a cumulation of one thousand mini decisions that snowballed into overwhelm. Existing in a state of constant overwhelm leads to the belief that you are not in control, that you can't push back, that you can't make it better.

I'm here to tell you that you *can*.

You probably can't eliminate all your night and weekend work immediately. It will take reflection, time, and practice. Just like the accumulation of more and more work, the shedding of work takes time. A commitment to putting writing at the center—a commitment to *yourself*—means that you'll start that process now.

Writing Drives Decisions about Content

Putting writing at the center of your career is not just good for your writing; it's good for your whole career. It gives you a way to focus your academic activities around a central idea. When you start to evaluate your activities through the lens of how they support your writing, you pull in activities that were disparate and scattered toward a central core. Your work stops feeling like you're pulled in a thousand directions and starts feeling like you're headed down a clear path. When I stopped teaching pre-basic English and aligned all my teaching with my research and writing, my teaching prep—selecting readings, reading student work, working out complex ideas about new takes on translanguaging—served a double purpose. It supported my teaching *and* my writing. Because of this, it made me a better teacher *and* a better writer.

Even when I taught a master's Research Methods in English Education course, I used the curriculum to delve deeper into my own research questions. Of course, I taught all the required themes for the course, but I used examples from my own research or research in translanguaging. When we talked about developing research questions for different methods, I created question examples about translanguaging.

If this sounds selfish to you or boastful, I invite you to reframe those patriarchy-planted thoughts. Making your area of research central to the course curriculum leverages your hard-won expertise. The energy you get from teaching what really gets you excited rubs off on students—and it makes you a better teacher.

Service is an area of your career that can often feel "tacked on." It is harder to align the content of service with your own writing and research, but it's not impossible. How could serving on a curriculum committee help you create programs that attract the perfect students to work with you? When I served on the graduate committee, I saw every incoming program application and volunteered to be the temporary advisor (a position we created to help orient students in their first semesters before they choose their thesis advisors) for any student I thought might be interested in the research area I was working on. Did we also have to do a lot of other things on the graduate committee that were less aligned? Sure. But by letting my writing drive my decisions about which committees I served on, all my committee work pulled a little bit closer to my central core. And that felt so much better than letting other people's expectations, or department "traditions," dictate my service work.

When you agree to mentor or supervise students, your writing must also drive those decisions. There are lots of reasons you might become the advisor of a graduate student other than them aligning with your area of expertise, particularly in the humanities and social sciences. You might be asked to serve as a reader on a graduate committee because of your research method expertise or your theoretical expertise, not your research subject area. Faculty of color are sought out by students of color for support beyond just their research subject area. The more the student's work aligns with your own work, however, the better job you'll do, and the better supervising and mentoring will feel. Reading students' thesis drafts, steering them through the literature, and helping them develop their ideas doubly supports your writing. Let your writing pull your student mentoring toward the center as well.

When writing becomes the organizing force driving your career, you feel more aligned. Your career becomes about *one thing*, and that allows you to do the deep work in your subject area you've been craving. Putting writing at the center of your career is a revolutionary, rebellious choice. It is radically pro-*you*.

Chapter 5:

The Myth of Accountability

(And What You Need Instead)

When academics join writing programs, they often say that they are searching for accountability. They think, "Oh good! Now I'll have accountability. That's what I really need: people around me to keep me in line."

Well, I'm here to tell you that **the idea that you need "accountability" to write is rooted in patriarchy**. This idea says that you are not to be trusted to complete work on your own. You are not to be trusted to set your own goals or meet your own deadlines. You are not to be trusted to prioritize yourself or your writing. Patriarchy is built on the mistrust of womxn. In the United States, for example, womxn could not open bank accounts or lines of credit without a male cosigner until the 1970s. We are not to be trusted with money! Since the 1990s, the number of cesarean births has tripled.[25] We are not to be trusted to push the baby out! We couldn't trust Hillary to be president because of emails!

Seriously, though, saying you need accountability to do things is distrusting *yourself*. If you are reading this book, you have already accomplished more than most people, and you didn't need someone prodding you along to do it. In *Playing Big*, Tara Mohr talks about discovering your inner mentor: "Though dressed in the guise of women's empowerment, all the encouragement for women to find the right mentors and right advice is often, underneath, the same old message telling them to turn away from their own intuitions and wisdom to privilege guidance coming from others instead."[26] To grow, to lead—to "play big," as Mohr puts it—you must learn to trust yourself. The endless search for "accountability" is based in a fundamental distrust in your ability to get writing done on your own.

Patriarchy can take the shape of paternalism. Besides being rooted in mistrust, the belief in the need for "accountability" to write also casts you as weak, in need of fatherly help. It says you are too weak to enforce your own boundaries, too weak to stand up for yourself, too weak to direct your career.

Of course, this is not accurate.

You are not weak. You are operating within a system that was not meant for you, and operating within that system causes self-doubt. It is utterly paternalistic to think that you would not get your writing done because you don't have some dominant figure there "holding you accountable," like a father watching the clock until curfew.

So, when you ask for accountability, you are buying into the idea that you are weak and not to be trusted.

You might be asking yourself, "Why haven't I been getting writing done, if it's not a lack of accountability?" Before now you didn't see all the ways in which academia is built to *deliberately keep you* from writing. Now that you see this, it's time to turn to the three things that you really need when you *think* you need accountability: self-trust, boundaries, and community. Instead of finding someone to "hold you accountable" to write, your work will be to trust yourself, hold your boundaries, and surround yourself with people inside of academia who also want to put writing at the center.

Developing Self-Trust

Julie, who I met when she joined our coaching program for mid-career professors, had served as a program director for years as an associate professor. She managed to keep her line of research going despite her administrative work, and she felt she was ready for—and frankly, deserved—a promotion. It was time for the university to recognize her hard work, dedication to her department, and strong scholarship; however, when she brought her case for promotion to the department committee, they turned her down. When Julie came to our coaching call, she was indignant. "I'm going to go over their heads to the dean," she told me. "And I am going to use all the energy

I have right now to compose the letter that will make my case for promotion despite not having my department's support."

I encouraged her to do just that. She left our call not certain whether she would actually submit that letter but very certain that it was the moment to write it. On our next call, Julie told me she had submitted that letter to the dean and that he would support her case for promotion. She was absolutely glowing with pride in herself for doing what she knew was right. She had trusted her inner mentor, and it felt amazing.

You can tap into that same trust by learning to listen to your intuition, to that gut feeling that pulls you to make certain choices. In online spaces, I often see academic womxn crowdsourcing big decisions about their careers: Should I go up for promotion early? Should I extend my tenure clock because of illness? Should I take this job or that job? I often want to reply, "Why are you asking an internet full of strangers about a decision that is so personal to you, so rooted in your deep desires and experiences, so central to who you are developing into as a scholar? Why not ask your inner voice, your inner mentor, instead?"

Writer Alexandra Frazen calls that inner intuitive voice your hut, your "head+gut ... the voice of instinct and intuition, that inexplicable feeling of what's right for you and you alone."[27] Instead of trusting others to guide you, or extrapolating from their experiences, you can trust your "hut" to lead you in the right direction.

As a writer (which is what you are, even if you don't primarily see yourself as one), you must listen to your inner mentor—your hut—and deeply, unwaveringly trust that voice. As womxn and nonbinary people, we are conditioned not to trust ourselves, to question our decisions and look outwardly for people to trust. Instead, I'm asking you to look inside. Frazen says that the hut "doesn't always speak in words. Sometimes it speaks in feelings, tingles, an invisible hand on your shoulder, a fire in your belly, tears in your eyes that won't stop." Trusting your hut means listening to these sensations and checking in with your hut deliberately and often. Just like in any relationship, trust in yourself is built over time.

Trusting that *you* are the best authority on *you* is key to a sustainable writing practice. Practicing listening to your inner mentor and consulting your hut will help you build that trust. The more you strengthen that self-trust, the less you will look outward for accountability. Instead, when you create a writing plan, you will trust that it is the best plan for you and implement it. You won't need external accountability because you will naturally be accountable to yourself. That doesn't mean you won't benefit from being surrounded by a supportive community (more on that later); it also doesn't mean you have to achieve your goals alone. What it does mean is that you have built the internal capacity to mentor yourself, to trust your hut. You become the greatest authority on your best interest.

Strength around Boundaries

When I met Brenda, she was a person with a lot of good problems. She had gotten tenure, was working at an institution she loved, and felt she was making a real difference in the lives of her students. But just two months after I started working with her in our mid-career coaching program, she got shoved into the spotlight as COVID-19 hit the United States. As an epidemiologist in public health, she became the leading authority on her campus and in her community for all things pandemic-related. Suddenly she had a regular spot on the local news and was getting called for media interviews multiple times a day. Local businesses started asking for her expertise when creating safety measures for their employees, and law firms began approaching her to consult for businesses they represented. Pre-COVID, Brenda had joined our program to figure out what the next stage in her career would look like, but it seemed like the outside world was deciding for her.

When the university president approached her about leading their COVID response team, Brenda decided to take control. To accomplish what her new, more visible position would allow her to do—which was exactly in line with her academic mission—she knew she needed strong boundaries. More than that, she knew she had to communicate those boundaries and negotiate for what she needed.

Before COVID, Brenda was granted a sabbatical for the next academic year. When she agreed to lead her campus' COVID response, she negotiated for a postponement of that sabbatical and for a complete release from all other service responsibilities while she led her university's COVID efforts. Brenda knew exactly what it would take to do what she wanted to do with the next phase of her career. She asked for what she wanted, erecting strong boundaries around her time and commitments, and was able to create the conditions for her success.

Brenda's boundaries were at the career level, but every day we must make choices to put up and hold boundaries if we are to protect our time so that we can do our work. We must draw a line in the sand for what is possible—and what is not—under our current workload and hold the line. Womxn and nonbinary people holding boundaries is just as radical as womxn and nonbinary people trusting themselves. When you put a date with your writing in your calendar and then hold that date firm, you are resisting the patriarchy that says you must please and accommodate.

At their core, boundaries are a kindness. They are a kindness to yourself and to others. When you say "no" to a student asking you to be on their committee because you truly don't have one more minute in your schedule, it is a kindness. Saying "yes" and then working overtime will make you resent both yourself and your student, and neither one of you deserves that. Boundaries are also a kindness because they teach others who look up to you how to act to preserve themselves, thus having more successful and fulfilling careers. And of course, boundaries preserve *you* so that you can do your work.

When I was an associate professor, I was inevitably asked to serve in departmental administration. I had been quite vocal about not wanting to be the chair, but I was convinced by my dearest colleagues to be the interim associate chair. In my department, "interim" could last for months or years, and frankly I was wary of the whole situation. I remember the former chair and the new chair, who I would serve with, looking at me with hopeful eyes as I considered their suggestion that I fill the role. They were both good friends and great leaders, and I thought I'd better lay down my boundaries right from the start. "Before I say 'yes,'" I told them, making eye contact with each one in turn, "I want you to know that I will save myself. I will not sacrifice my mental or physical well-being for this department. If things look bad, I will not hesitate to jump ship and let it sink."

Harsh? Maybe.

True? Absolutely.

Well, it maybe was not quite as true in practice. I said yes, and both my physical and mental health suffered.

It was a slow deterioration. I was determined to keep my research line going, and I had a funded project with research assistants collecting data. But I was also teaching and, most importantly, learning how the heck to do my new job, which now required me to be physically present in the office all day most days.

First breakfast slipped, then lunch. In the morning rush of getting kids to school and getting to the office on time, I stopped eating breakfast and packing lunch, so I ate greasy cafeteria food twice a day. I gained twenty pounds that year. I stopped working out, insisting there was no time, so I suffered from back and wrist problems that were kept at bay with my previous light exercise routine.

But the mental weight of the job was the worst. My responsibilities included reviewing all the English majors' transcripts to both advise them and make sure that the seniors had met graduation requirements. It was a lot of spreadsheets, a lot of GPA calculation, and too much paperwork that, if I got it wrong, would alter a young person's life. There was also constant fighting amongst faculty, a hiring freeze on replacing our departmental secretary, and nasty emails critiquing all kinds of trivial aspects of our efforts to lead the department. The potential to lead and make change was there, but it was like trying to run with ankle weights on. While carrying a sack full of cats.

In the end, I lasted just one academic year. All the big talk about "saving myself," the boundaries I tried to set at the beginning? They did not hold. I did not hold them. But I did learn an important lesson during my short stint in admin.

Just like the sum of your days equals your life, the sum of your everyday work activities equals your career.

I realized in that admin position that I hated the everyday activities. I hated the paperwork and the exploding faculty members. I hated the GPA calculation spreadsheets and the short-sightedness of upper administration. I looked at my daily activities and thought, "What does this add up to?" Your daily activities *are* your career, so what would my career be if I stayed in admin? It would be a ton of paperwork plus frustrated dreams.

My foray into admin was a good lesson about boundaries. I thought I had them. The reason I got out after just one year was that I realized I couldn't hold those boundaries. And that lack of control over boundaries meant that my days were spent doing mostly what I didn't want to do, instead of mostly what I wanted to do. That's the key about boundaries: they allow you to create your career on your terms. Your career is the sum of the activities you do day-to-day.

Writing sessions add up to publications, and publications add up to influence. They add up to your voice. Your impact. Boundaries let you define how you spend your days, thus how you shape your career. Just as self-trust must be practiced, so must erecting and holding boundaries. It takes time to hold boundaries well and consistently. But you can do it, and you are not alone.

Community over Accountability

The culture of academia paints the image of the professor as a "lone wolf." Particularly in the social sciences and humanities, the predominate image is the tweed-clad, crazy-haired, glasses-wearing professor alone in his book-stuffed office until all hours. Of course, there are research teams, particularly in STEM fields, but academia does not have a culture that promotes asking for and receiving help.

Instead, there is a pervasive "if you're smart enough, you'll figure it out" mentality.

This is precisely why community in academia is a radical idea. Womxn and nonbinary people in community together is an even more radical idea because that act of solidarity—of lifting each other up, of standing together and getting your voice heard in an academic culture that is structured to devalue you—is powerful.

It is more powerful than the paternalistic idea that you need "accountability." Coming together and supporting each other in developing self-trust and holding firm boundaries beats "accountability" every day of the week.

The connection between searching for accountability and finding, instead, community came from Dr. Felicia Thomas, who joined one of our academic writing retreats. On that retreat, she said, "I thought I needed accountability, but what I really needed was community." The idea of seeking accountability in writing always rubbed me the wrong way. But when Felicia said that sentence, it shifted how I saw the importance of community for academic writing.

So much about academia is lonely—or painted to be. To be sure, there are many lonely days in the library. Reading is very solitary, and writing can be too. Writing your dissertation is the first lonely act. You must do it by yourself, even though academics who do lab work know that they are never truly doing an experiment alone. But the words on the page must come from your brain, and yours alone. Part of the solitude of writing is in that act of getting something out of your head and onto the page. It's between you and the blinking cursor, and that can feel very lonely. We learn from the beginning of our academic training that when we write, we write alone.

The solitary nature of writing is reinforced throughout your career. The tenure system values "solo-authored publications" above all else. Even if you are coauthoring a paper, you are not usually in the same room writing at the same time. Coauthoring is often like playing "hot potato," passing a draft from author to author, chipping away at sections. Coauthoring rarely feels like community or togetherness. At best, it feels like collaboration, which is not quite the same as community.

Developing a true writing community is a radical idea. Communities share experiences, but they also share values.

The solitary nature of writing is sometimes why keeping a date with your writing is difficult. It's just too easy to walk away or do something else. But embedded within a community of writers who value writing time, self-trust, and boundaries, the decision to stay and write is easier.

Such a community is the very opposite of academic culture, which values busyness, overwork, and solitude. Pushing back against the culture of academia that paternalistically tells you that you need accountability becomes resistance as you embrace community.

Because of this, writing *together* is a radical idea. In May 2020, my company began a big experiment: What would happen if we developed a community of womxn and nonbinary academics whose core purpose was to write together? Would writing side-by-side via Zoom be powerful enough to help participants learn to keep that date with their writing? Could community, built well and with the shared values of self-trust and boundaries, beat out accountability? Turns out members liked hanging out together, even in silence. Our Zoom writing meetings, where we simply shared goals in the chat and checked in with each other before signing off, were enough to develop the community so many of us long for in academia. When you have found or created a community that shares your values, you no longer need "accountability" in the traditional sense.

Rebellious Reflections

1. Think about a moment in your life when you deeply trusted yourself, in any context. What made you sure you were doing the right thing? What did it feel like when that self-trust paid off? How can you leverage the memory of that self-trust to trust yourself more when it comes to writing?

2. Can you identify just one boundary around your time, energy, or attention that you often let slip? What is one small step that you can take to hold that boundary? Who might support you in that step?

3. Who are your best, most supportive colleagues? Who in your community can you connect with who shares the same desires to make time to write? What is one simple way you could begin to build community with those people?

Part 3:

RESISTING "SHOULDS"

Chapter 6:
Stop "Shoulding" Yourself

I n 2017, I started a Facebook group called *I Should Be Writing*. At its largest, the group had 16,000 members. It was a place where womxn and nonbinary people in academia came together to honestly ask questions and find community support around writing. About once every six weeks, we get a post like this:

> *"How does everyone deal with feelings of inadequacy when hearing the good news of colleagues' publishing success? It is so difficult for me not to compare my own productivity to my peers, and I end up feeling inadequate."*

These posts usually get a rush of comments because the original poster has struck a chord with group members.

"I feel this too. I also just try to focus on my own successes, but it's hard."

"I publish a decent amount, but I am constantly comparing myself to the superstar from my cohort who publishes like four to eight articles a year. She has already published six in 2021!!"

Whether you're looking to your PhD cohort, your current colleagues, or some kind of imaginary standard, the pull to compare how much you're writing and publishing to how much other people are writing and publishing is strong. In the last chapter, we talked about how lonely academia can be, often by design. The emphasis that academic culture puts on solo ideas, solitary strength, and the "lone wolf" scholar naturally leads to comparison, particularly because you have no idea what is going on behind the outward signs of others' "productivity."

The hidden nature of the process behind people's academic struggles and achievements leads to a distorted sense of what we "should" do. This "shoulding" is reinforced by a system that is intentionally unclear about what "enough" writing and publishing looks like.

If what constitutes "enough" writing and publishing is never outlined explicitly in tenure and promotion requirements or job descriptions, then it is logical to look around and try to divine what we should do based on what others are doing. But the problem with this comparison game is that you can never win because you are never comparing apples to apples. You never know what kind of support the other scholar has at home or at work, the physical and mental health challenges or advantages the person has. You don't know how many hours a day they work, or how many courses they teach to how many students, so the inevitable result of your comparison is what the post above expresses: feelings of inadequacy.

Not surprisingly, feeling inadequate is not going to inspire you to write or publish more. In fact, it will hinder your ability to do so. The comparison game robs you of writing. Your mind creates a long list of what you "should" be doing, but that list is only based on what you *imagine* other people are doing that you're not. Your list of "shoulds" is distorted.

Not only that but also the "shoulds" of academic culture are contradictory. You should network and collaborate; at the same time, you should have single-authored publications. You should strive for inquiry and innovation, but you shouldn't rock the boat before tenure. You should be on a quest for new, original ideas, but you should be able to figure things out for yourself. You should write every day, but you should keep your email response time under two hours. You should be so passionate about your work that you would do it for free, but you should aggressively seek grant funding. Surely there can't be a clear set of "shoulds" if so many of them are in direct competition with each other.

What if I told you that your success as a writer, your ability to become a prolific publisher, cannot be found in anyone else's behind-the-scenes story or in the contradictory shoulds of academic culture?

Your ability to write and publish more has nothing to do with what you *think* you should be doing and has everything to do with **figuring out who you are and what works for you—and then leaning into that**.

Know Thyself

You already have everything you need to develop a writing practice that will sustain your career. You don't have to develop new habits or learn new tips or tricks. What you need to do to write and publish enough is to know yourself and then trust that self-knowledge. Earlier in this book, I walked through the process of understanding your Soaring State: that time of day when you feel energized and driven in your work. I asked you to listen to what your body and mind were feeling each hour of the day and record that in a journal to figure out when your Soaring State is, and equally important, when your Slogging State is. (Remember that you can find this exercise and more in the free PDF workbook that accompanies this book at https://www.cathymazak.com/workbook). Then I told you that just one to two hours of writing once or twice a week during your Soaring State would be enough to see a marked difference in the amount of writing you got done and, more importantly, the positive feelings about your writing that I want you to develop. That process is a process of self-knowing.

You can (and should) repeat this process of self-knowing for all the practices you are trying to develop. The basic process looks like this: (1) observe yourself by taking notes on how you work, (2) draw conclusions about what works best for you based on the observational data you collected *with no judgment about what you "should" be like*, and (3) implement changes that take advantage of what is working.

Learning to observe without judgment is key in this process. Judgment usually comes in the form of "shoulds": I should be able to work faster, I should write more words per minute, I should be able to do this without going back to the readings. But as we've established above, "shoulds" are unreliable and inconsistent. You cannot trust the "shoulds." You can trust the process of self-knowing through observation without judgment.

One of the questions I get asked the most in my work as an academic writing coach is about how to break writing projects into tasks. How big should a writing task be? How can I estimate the time it will take me to do a task? Do tasks all need to be the same size? How granular should I go?

These are important questions to ask *yourself*.

Most of the time these questions come from thinking there is one way that you should be breaking projects into tasks, as if there is some secret way to break writing projects into tasks that is the correct way, the way you *should* do it.

The truth is that there is only a way that works for you, not a way that works for everybody.

You can use the process of self-knowing to figure out how best to break writing projects into tasks. I've mapped out this observational process as a handout in the free PDF workbook that accompanies this book at https://www.cathymazak.com/workbook.

1. **Observe:** Choose a writing project (a journal article, book chapter, etc.). Write your working title at the top of the page, then list all the tasks needed to complete it. Release the idea that there is a perfect way to do this. This process will teach you *your* perfect way, so don't overthink it and just write a big list. Then create a table with three columns: the task, how long you plan for it to take, and how long it actually took. Fill out the first two columns. As you work through your task list, fill out the last column of your chart.

2. **Draw conclusions:** Analyze your table. Did you consistently overestimate the time it took you to complete a task? Underestimate? Did you find some task sizes to be okay, some to be too granular, some to be too big? Note all of this without judgment. Write a few sentences that capture your conclusions, like: "It consistently takes me twice the time I plan for to complete a task."

3. **Implement changes:** If you found it takes you twice as long as you thought to finish most tasks, then the next time you write you should double the predicted task completion time. If you found that breaking tasks down too granularly was over-

whelming, next time you should stick to slightly bigger tasks. Write down the changes you'll try next time so that you don't forget.

Notice that the "shoulds" mentioned in step three are now *your* shoulds based on data, not imagined shoulds or culturally mandated shoulds. **Self-knowing is the process of finding what works for you and leaning in.**

This book is my first solo-authored book, the first work of this length for which I needed to write every single word. My biggest fear around writing it was being able to write enough words to fill a book, to be able to sustain that much writing. If you've ever heard my podcast, you know that I have plenty of things to say, so the fear that I wouldn't have enough to say to fill a book seems humorous in retrospect. But, no judgment, that was my fear. I used the process of self-knowing to build confidence— and a plan—for meeting my six-month deadline. I spent a good amount of time planning and outlining, felt that the book had a solid structure, and was ready to write all those words.

In my previous work writing academic articles and edited volumes, I always preferred a task list approach. But I knew with this project I needed to tackle my fear of writing enough words head-on, so I took a different approach. First, I observed how many words I could write in one Soaring Session, using my premade outline as a guide. I noticed that "one session" for me meant ninety minutes. After that, I started to lose energy. So, I observed how many words I could write in one ninety-minute Soaring Session. After observing for three or four sessions, I realized that I could write between five hundred and 750 words per session consistently.

Hold up! Did you just compare yourself to me? Did you just think, "OMG that's fast! Should I be writing at that speed?"

Stop. Right. Now. You just fell into the shoulding trap.

Remember, you can't compare yourself to others because you're almost always comparing apples to oranges. The kind of writing I'm doing is writing that comes out of my own head onto the page based on an outline. If you compare this kind of writing to integrating sources while crafting a scholarly argument or creating the graphs and diagrams necessary for scientific writing, it is a false comparison.

You also don't know my circumstances. I'm writing during my Soaring State, which I know well, and there is a babysitter keeping my children from interrupting me. You can't compare my speed to your speed if you are writing while parenting or sitting in your office where colleagues can knock on the door.

And anyway, *what I do doesn't matter*. What YOU do matters.

Back to my process. Having observed how I work and drawn conclusions, I created a work plan that leveraged my observations and data. I went through my calendar and blocked off ninety-minute writing sessions. I did this taking into account the activities and commitments that were already scheduled on my calendar. Some weeks I could fit in three sessions, others just one or two. Then I made a spreadsheet with the following columns: chapter title, words written, goal word count, number of writing sessions needed, drafted by date, and notes. (You can see my chart in the workbook that accompanies this book, which you can download for free at https://www.cathymazak. com/workbook). The goal word count column was based on my total goal word count (the one I told the publisher) divided by the nine chapters I outlined. I filled in the rows for the two chapters that I had already drafted for the book proposal. I took the "goal word count" for the rest of the chapters, divided it by the 500-750 words per session I observed, and came up with a "number of sessions" it would take to write each chapter. Then I went back to my calendar and filled in the "drafted by date" based on the number of sessions I knew I needed and when they were scheduled. According to this plan, I could completely draft this book in about four months, leaving me two months for developmental and copy editing.

Despite the extensive planning, I always know that things won't go exactly according to plan. As I draft this book, I continue to collect data about myself and refine my time and word count estimations. After each writing session, I update the "actual word count" in the spreadsheet. I do this without judgment. Whether I hit my goals or not, it is data.

> Self-knowing gives me the power of predict-
> ing my writing project accurately, and pre-
> dictability is better than shoulds.

Let me say that again: your goal is to establish a predictable writing practice, not to establish a writing practice based on other people's shoulds. If your writing practice is predictable, you continue to foster a good relationship with your writing, which means you will have a sustainable practice. If you can predict how long a writing project will take you, you can more easily project-plan it and stop relying on self-imposed deadlines that you always miss. Predictability gives you power and makes you effective. Predictability is better than apples to oranges productivity comparisons.

I use the same process I used to predict my book writing timeline with my clients. Ariana was excited to project-plan her first book with me. But unlike my book project (this book), Ariana's project was a book version of her dissertation. She had a book contract signed, and she didn't have to worry about words on the page. What she had to worry about was revising each chapter, adding updated analysis, and cutting dissertation overexplaining. She was already worried that she would not make her publisher's deadline and had even reached out to the editor to ask for an extension, even though the deadline was still six months away.

I asked her, "How long does it take you to revise a chapter?"

When she replied, "I don't know! I haven't started," I walked her through the process of self-knowing.

Ariana had no concrete way to predict whether she would actually need an extension or not until she did step one of the self-knowing process to figure out how long it took her (roughly) to revise a chapter or a section. Once she realized that she was in control of her work plan, that she could predict—based on data!—how long her book revision would take, she was so much more confident and relaxed.

To Thine Own Self Be True

The process of self-knowing is a process of doing more of what works for you. It is not about anyone else. It is not about expert ideas or best practices.

It's not totally surprising if this seems like an unusual way to increase productivity. Most of the time we're taught that when we're not good at something we need to work hard to learn to do it better. We focus time and effort on learning what we're *not* good at.

I'm asking you to focus time and effort on learning what you *are* good at.

If you were bad at math in school and great at history, then maybe you spent more hours studying math, or stayed after school for extra math tutoring. That approach was probably one that worked for you in school. But now, as a scholar, you should do the opposite: if you're bad at math and good at history, do more history.

The same goes for writing. If writing five hundred words a day no matter what doesn't work for you but going into the office on Saturday morning when no one is there makes the writing flow, then build your writing practice around Saturday mornings. If waking up an hour before the rest of your house to write makes you resent writing but writing as soon as you get to your office pre-email-checking makes you feel like the master of your destiny, then first-thing-in-the-workday writing it is. If writing at 4:30 a.m. works for you and you love it, then do that!

You will not increase your productivity (writing or otherwise) by adopting tips, tricks, and hacks that were developed for other people. You will increase your productivity through the process of self-knowing and then leaning in.

Rebellious Reflections

1. What are the "shoulds" that you currently believe about writing in academia? Make a big list! Now destroy the list.

2. Does it usually take you longer or shorter to complete writing tasks than you think? How do you feel about that? Have your feelings changed in light of this chapter?

3. How can you start to identify patterns in your workflows and then lean into them? What parts of your writing workflow do you think you "shouldn't" do (e.g., read for "too long" before writing)? How could those patterns actually be your secret sauce or work to your advantage?

Resisting "Shoulds"

There are a thousand ways to do academia. It is a radical choice to do it *your* way.

Comparing yourself to others or sitting in unkind judgment of your own practices will not help you write and publish more. The list of "shoulds" is long and contradictory. It is also unreliable and unhelpful.

Imagine instead tens of thousands of academic womxn and nonbinary people, including you, approaching their careers firmly rooted in their own self-knowing. What an act of resistance that would be.

Chapter 7:
When Writing Gets Derailed

By May 2018, I'd had a bit of a year. It had been a little over a year since the four-month-long student strikes began at the University of Puerto Rico in March 2017, where I was a tenured, full professor. It was a trying time for everyone. We didn't know what to expect from day to day. The public sentiment against the students, who were fighting against severe budget cuts that would potentially collapse the university, revealed a deeper misunderstanding and indifference to public higher education in general. It made everyone—students and professors—question what exactly we were doing at the University of Puerto Rico, for whom, and why.

When the strike ended in June 2017, we had to finish the remainder of the semester. Then we started the new semester right up again in August, with the budget cuts still looming, sitting on pins and needles every day with nothing resolved. It was a volatile environment.

And then Hurricane Maria hit on September 20, 2017.

Even typing its name makes me well up. It is still both painful and also oddly beautiful to think of those days. There was so much destruction and suffering but also so much community togetherness. My family spent a week clearing our road so that we could get out. It was amazing to be together like that, with a common mission (and no internet!), but it was painful to know that our neighbors and countless others had lost their homes, many their lives, and that my parents and sister had to watch from afar. I couldn't communicate with them to tell them that we were okay.

Our university, in Mayagüez, reopened about a month later. With that came the struggles to teach and learn without consistent power, when just getting food and water was a daily struggle, with a library that had been destroyed and students who had lost their homes.

It was hard to finish that semester, which we finally did at the end of January 2018 (with just a few days of winter break). But somehow finishing the second semester, which ran from February to June 2018, was even harder. By May, things were much more stable. Though the library was still closed, power was consistent, grocery stores were full again, and life in the community surrounding the university in Mayagüez was "normal." But even so, I was not normal.

In May 2018, I recognized that I was about to burn out. I say "about to" because my body had been giving me signals that I needed to slow way down and make some changes, but I had not been completely knocked on my butt—yet. I "only" felt exhausted from the moment I woke up to the moment I went to bed. My normal burst of morning energy (my Soaring State) was fleeting or non-existent. I felt mentally foggy. I couldn't find the words for things immediately. I felt on the verge of tears (more than usual!). Because I had experienced burnout before, I recognized what was happening and took action to make it to the end of the semester without actually burning out. I forced myself to rest, to go to bed when the kids went to bed, to eliminate absolutely everything "extra" from both work and home obligations. Then I planned my summer as a recovery from the year, rather than time to "get ahead."

The academic year plows on, and we are expected to plow on with it. Despite budget cuts, student strikes, devastating hurricanes, and global pandemics, we go on. We go on teaching the students, sitting on the committees, gathering the data, writing the papers.

The pace feels relentless, and the message is: *keep up.* The pace of the academic year gives little time for pause or recovery. Even the "breaks" are meant to be catch-up times. I often joke that academics feel like anything is possible in May. The summer is shiny and new, full of possibilities for "clearing your plate" or "getting ahead with writing."

But of course, the summer never pans out exactly how you expect it's going to, and by August, dreams of writing projects checked off your list are dashed, and the relentless year starts again.

Throughout it all there is an expectation that your productivity will remain the same, steady despite anything else going on in your life or the world. "Sameness" in production is an expectation of fast capitalism, and it is profoundly ableist. It is a patriarchal expectation, based on a "normal" worker: a male with an at-home support system to buffer him against the effects of his child's illness, supporting his needs to eat and sleep as he plows through the work. But the individual, ultimately, is responsible for maintaining their own steady level of production. When you lose motivation or get off track, *you* are to blame, not the system that ignores context while expecting production to remain the same.

Never was this more obvious to every academic than during the COVID-19 pandemic. Despite small children at home, despite ill family members, despite a haphazard move to online teaching in the spring of 2020, the message from most universities to both faculty and students was a chilly: *plow on*. The collective level of stress among academics with school-aged children was palpable during every call for every online training I did throughout 2020—and well into 2021. Some universities offered tenure clock extensions, but they didn't offer tenure requirement reductions. Extending the clock only means extending the stress and delaying the pay raise and stability.

I had a coaching client who contracted COVID and didn't even bother to tell her university. She just kept trying to deliver her online classes, because what was the point? They couldn't do anything to help her, in her view. Best to plow on.

The truth is that just like life, the academic year ebbs and flows. There are predictable ebbs and flows, like the midterm and end-of-term grading rush, and unpredictable disruptions, like a sudden illness or a global pandemic. To expect sameness throughout the academic year, every year, is oppression. It ignores the context in which we serve our students and collect our data; it ignores our humanity. For womxn, who shoulder a disproportionate amount of the care burden in families and communities, expecting academic production to remain steady throughout all ebbs and flows and disruptions is particularly demeaning. What's worse is that womxn and nonbinary people blame themselves for not being able to keep their motivation up or their academic production steady, as if they are not part of a larger system of patriarchal, fast-capitalist oppression.

Two major problems haunt academics trying to change their writing practice: "derailing" events (i.e., disruptions at work or home that take over and drop writing back down to the bottom of the list) and a perceived lack of motivation. Both lead to a feeling of failure, often accompanied by negative self-talk that sounds like: "Why can't I just get shake off the funk and finish the project?" or "I got derailed by X months ago and I can't figure out why I'm still not caught up." At their core, these problems expect production to remain the same despite everything else going on. Instead of accepting that expectation, we must ride the ebbs and flows and treat the disruptions for what they are: often traumatic life events that deserve an appropriate recovery period. Rises and dips in motivation are part of being human. Our motivation does not remain constant on all projects all the time. When you shed the expectation of sameness and steadiness, you will not only be happier but you are also far more likely to maintain your writing practice.

Riding Academia's Ebbs and Flows

Before looking at how derailing events and lack of motivation affect your writing practice, I want to dig into academia's predictable ebbs and flows. Whether your university is on a semester system, trimester system, or quarter system, the academic year has predictable ups and downs. The oppressive expectation of sameness makes these predictable ebbs and flows stressful. Here's a common pattern that I experienced teaching during a semester system:

Prior to Week 1: I'm going to get all my ducks in a row so when we start classes in one week, I am ahead!

Day 1: I didn't get as far ahead as I wanted, but I still feel good!

Weeks 1–5: My optimism about how this semester will be less stressful decreases each week.

Weeks 6–10: I'm starting to feel stressed out. I bring work home on weekends (not doing that work but bringing it back and forth with me each weekend).

Weeks 11–15: *The semester hits the fan.*

Semester Break: I plan on finally getting to all those projects I put off during weeks 6–15, but I can't because I'm completely exhausted.

And the next semester, it would all start over again. I'd feel guilty for not sustaining my writing practice through it all, overwhelmed by work, and constantly behind. I'd get to the "break" but never feel like I could really rest.

Does this sound like a familiar pattern? You blame yourself for inconsistency: "Why can't I keep my writing practice going throughout the semester? What's wrong with me?"

There's nothing wrong with you!

What's wrong is thinking that we should maintain "sameness" while working in a system with predictable ebbs and flows. Instead of striving for sameness, riding the ebbs and flows is a more effective approach. One of the benefits of a writing system based on Soaring Sessions is that you can maintain writing throughout the ebbs and flows, but dial it back. Just one Soaring Session a week keeps your writing projects alive through the times when the semester hits the fan.

And even in the worst-case scenario, the sustainable, relationship-based approach to writing described in the third chapter can also support you through stopping your writing practice completely and then restarting it without guilt.

Yes, I just said *stopping your writing practice completely*.

I do not believe in writing no matter what, because I never could. So, if you're looking for permission to hit the pause button on your writing practice, here it is. In fact, I think that lowering your expectations around writing or putting it aside completely is a very healthy way to respond to the semester's ebbs and flows. That's exactly what Soaring Sessions can do for you.

Remember, your relationship with writing is the most important thing. If hanging on to your writing practice through predictably stressful moments in the semester grounds you and gives you a joyful respite from the whirling stress of the semester's peak, then keep writing. If trying to write during the worst times of the semester causes you to feel stress and overwhelm, then don't do it. Trying to write no matter what can make you resent writing, and that will damage your relationship-based writing system. Instead, ride the ebbs and flows.

Even if you are a newbie academic only one year into your PhD program when you're reading this, you can predict when the semester gets hairy. Instead of pretending that those hairy moments shouldn't matter, what if you adapted your writing practice around them?

Here's what adjusting your writing practice to adapt to the semester's predictable ebbs and flows looks like. Look at your calendar for the events that cause the ebbs and flows: the week your ninety students turn in midterm exams or papers, the week before a conference presentation proposal is due, the week before a grant is due, the week you're in school and your kids are off (because why can't spring breaks ever line up?), the end of semester flood of requests for recommendation letters, the week before final grades are due. I like to mark these times in yellow in my calendar as "caution weeks." It's a way of saying to myself: "Hey! You know you get busy around this time, so take it easy and be gentle with yourself."

During those "caution weeks" I might dial back my number of writing sessions to just one Soaring Session on a Monday. I might even decide to eliminate all my writing sessions during particularly stressful times. Think of it as putting a pin in your writing practice. But here's the key: write into your calendar when you'll unpin it again.

There's a big difference between deliberately choosing to pause your writing in response to predictable ebbs and flows and letting the semester bowl right over your writing. The first is an intentional decision, one that you control, one that you make to honor yourself, your health, and your writing.

Yes, it honors your writing to decide
to pause your practice!

It proactively preserves your relationship with writing. Remember what we learned in the last chapter: predictable is better than "productive." By responding to the ebbs and flows of the semester, you are creating the predictability that will lead, ultimately, to more writing.

Surviving Derailing Events

While there are always the predictable ebbs and flows, sometimes the disruptions in your semester are unpredictable. I call these "derailing events" because that's how most academic womxn and nonbinary people I work with describe them. Derailing events feel like being blindsided and often cause us to drop our writing practice completely—and rightfully so.

Derailing events can be personal like your own illness or global like the Black Lives Matter fight for racial justice. No matter the cause, the effect is lack of concentration, throwing our carefully constructed schedules out the window, and, if not handled carefully, burnout.

When I experienced one of these derailing events, I didn't know how to respond, and it almost led me to check myself into the hospital. About two weeks into the semester after I came back from my second maternity leave, my ten-month-old son stopped breathing. I was nursing him to sleep in a chair in his darkened baby room, practically falling asleep myself, when he suddenly sat up, vomited, and turned a horrible shade of grey.

The next fifteen minutes were a panicked blur. I pulled my three-year-old out of bed and made her put shoes on with her princess nightgown. My husband was just arriving home from work, and I remember screaming at him that we needed to get to the hospital while I ducked under the garage door, which couldn't open fast enough.

My son was breathing again as I strapped him into the car seat, but he was still that awful ashy gray/blue. We arrived at the hospital, and I scooped him up and ran to the desk. I remember how calm everyone was. No one was rushing to take his vitals. No one came to help. I had to sign in and take a number while my baby flopped in my arms and continued to vomit.

This was the beginning of the ten most horrible days of my life.

If you've ever tried to sleep in a hospital, you understand my level of exhaustion. Over the course of ten days, I only went home for maybe an hour at a time when my husband would stay at the hospital so that I could shower and eat. The rules at the only children's hospital in western Puerto Rico mandated that the mother stay overnight with the patient. Plus, I was still breastfeeding, so it was really only me who could stay.

It was the second week of classes. My husband and I were both pretenure. It was 2010, and I didn't have a smartphone, so there was really nothing I could do. I think I called the department and just told them that I was in the hospital with the baby until further notice. All thoughts of the semester dissolved in the blurry exhaustion of caring for the sick kiddo (who was doing better but needed almost constant breathing treatments).

When we were finally released from the hospital, I jumped back into the semester with both feet. I was running a large grant project and teaching three first-year English classes. It was more-than-full-time work.

But as soon as I got home from work it was medicines and breathing treatments, coaxing kids to bed, then crashing myself, only to be woken up at least twice a night by a sniffly baby. I felt like I was on a treadmill set five clicks too fast, and I couldn't get off it or slow it down. Brain fog was seriously affecting my work, but I was completely in survival mode and hardly noticed.

By late October, I was breaking down. One day I was sitting in my driveway, the transition zone between "day job" and "all night job," talking on the phone with my sister about hospitalizing myself. I was crying, saying I couldn't keep up the pace. "Don't you have sick leave you can take?" she asked.

"I couldn't possibly do that! It's like week ten of the semester. What would happen to my classes? And my grant project?" I moaned.

But in that moment, my smart sister made it clear: take action or end up in the hospital yourself.

So, I took sick leave. Right at the worst time of the semester. I remember sitting in my department head's office. At the time he was young and single, and I remember feeling like he would never understand, or that he would push back. He didn't.

I took my doctor's note to human resources, and I went home and slept. For two weeks I dropped off the kids at daycare and went home and forced myself to lie down. I didn't check email. I didn't try to get writing done. I just deliberately rested.

And despite all my internal resistance and guilt, I realized: "I *can* possibly." I realized that the university didn't stop without me. My classes didn't even stop! The program manager of my grant never even knew I was gone. My Co-PI swiftly managed everything in my absence, as she had when I was on maternity.

When I had to miss the second week of classes to be in the hospital with my son, I didn't blink an eye. But when I needed to take a leave to prevent ending up in the hospital myself, I said, "I couldn't possibly."

In May 2018, at the end of the traumatic academic year when Maria changed all of our lives, I almost broke down again. That time it was different. We were a country exhausted from hurricane recovery, a university trying to find our footing under blow after blow by the *junta*, threatening to cut our budget into nonexistence. We were collectively breaking down.

But that time I recognized the signals and took action sooner. It heard the desperate voice in my head that said, "I can't keep this up. If I could only rest …" I listened to her, and I deliberately rested. On the weekends I made myself lie down. I cleared my schedule so that I didn't have to leave the house. We ate more take-out (I called it "outsourcing dinner"), and the kids watched more Netflix.

I whittled down my to-do list until it only contained the absolutely necessary items to finish the semester: Grade the papers. Give the classes. *That's it.* I excused myself from faculty meetings and from meetings of all kinds (And I wasn't the only one; no one had the energy for meetings.).

The difference between this almost-breakdown and the first one was that I truly believed "I *can* possibly."

I knew that even if I cut way back everything would still be fine. The world would not end. At the same time, I deeply understood that if I didn't deliberately rest, I would collapse, and *that* wouldn't serve anyone.

If you are faced with a derailing event—either personal or collective—you might react like I did initially and think that you can't possibly stop. This thought stems from the oppressive insistence on sameness and steadiness that academia socializes. Many academics who must take leave feel shame around that, embarrassed that they "couldn't keep up." But there is no shame in being human, and derailing events certainly remind us of our humanity. Academia can be soul-sucking. It can be all-consuming. But you do not have to be consumed. You can stop.

Just like when adjusting to predictable ebbs and flows, a writing system that can pause and restart is essential for dealing with unpredictable derailing events. The expectation of anything less is ridiculous and oppressive.

Derailing *Academic* Events

Sometimes derailing events aren't personal or public; they are academic. For example, you might have a great flow going on an article and—boom—you receive a revise and resubmit. Or your graduate student, who is scrambling to meet the dissertation deadline so she can defend this semester, turns in a chapter two weeks later than you were expecting it. Or the dean calls and asks you to drop everything to represent her at a meeting about the new program you are developing.

These kinds of events can derail your writing, but the solution to these kinds of *academic* derailments is different than for illnesses or natural disasters.

Academic derailments are part of the job, but they become much less problematic when you have firm boundaries, systems, and processes. Just like predicting the semester's ebbs and flows and adjusting your expectations around them, you can create boundaries, systems, and processes to mitigate the effect of academic derailments. Again, the point is to predict what you can. By nature, we don't know when an academic derailment might happen (that's unpredictable), but we do know that these types of events will happen (*that* is predictable). Revise and resubmits, student work being late, and surprise meetings are part of your job as an academic. But you can control how you handle those academic disruptions so that they don't feel like disruptions.

For example, if your student misses an agreed-upon deadline for you to review her work, then the next date that she gets to have her work reviewed by you is the next scheduled time for that activity in your calendar. You need: (1) a system for scheduling review of student work that you communicate to the student and block on your calendar; (2) a process for when the student misses your deadline (she must wait until the next time you have review of student work scheduled on your calendar, i.e., you don't adjust your calendar based on her lateness); and (3) firm boundaries to hold tight to the systems and processes you created so they actually work. In the free PDF workbook that accompanies this book, I've included an exercise for you to create these systems and processes for the usual academic derailments that you face. You can grab the workbook at https://www.cathymazak.com/workbook.

The Solution to Lack of Motivation in Writing is Rest

Whether you are facing predictable (ebbs and flows) or unpredictable (derailing events) disruptions in your semester and your writing practice, those disruptions often result in a self-proclaimed "lack of motivation." I hear this from my clients all the time: "I have no motivation to finish this project, what can I do?" or "I finally have time to write, but I have no motivation."

One of my clients, Anna, came to a group coaching call with just that problem. "I just can't seem to do anything," she lamented. "I have zero motivation to work on my writing." Anna had given birth to twins during the COVID-19 pandemic. They were about three months old at the time of our call. She had limited childcare along with a three-year-old!

I looked her in the eyes (via Zoom) and said, "It is time for you NOT to 'do.' It is time for you to rest." I asked her to tell me three things that were on her calendar that she could *not* do that week. And I emphasized that she would need to replace those items with *nothing*.

When we are exhausted, when we have been through a derailing event or a busy time in the semester, *of course* we feel a lack of motivation to keep writing. Though we often read a lack of motivation as an internal flaw or a problem with the individual project, it is usually just an indication that you are tired. This is why you get to the end of a particularly trying semester and you can't "catch up" on your writing, even though you technically have time over break. You are spent. There is no place to write from. You need to rest (which is exactly what the next chapter is about).

I had the great fortune of working with Martha-Beck-trained life coach Natalie Miller. One of the things she taught me that has stuck with me the most is about the relationship between creation and restoration. Natalie explained that Western culture puts a lopsided emphasis on creation and production: work five days a week, rest two; work fifty weeks a year, vacation two weeks. We are expected to sustain this high amount of work without the appropriate counterweight of restoration and rest. What's worse, when we want to create or produce more (more writing, for example), we think that we should spend more hours creating when instead, you actually need to restore and rest more to support more creation.

This understanding of the relationship between creation and restoration is important when facing a lack of motivation. Lack of motivation is the natural result of both predictable and unpredictable semester disruptions. When you are trying to make your way through disruptions, you are often not restoring yourself appropriately to support creation because you are striving to make your production (even in your most disrupted periods) look the same all the time. This is the fast-capitalist, patriarchal, ableist expectation, after all. But of course, you come through one of these disrupted periods with what you describe as a lack of motivation, an inability to muster the energy to get your work done.

After my son's stay at the hospital, and my subsequent two-week leave, I still could not write. In fact, I was still so burned out that my family intervened. My husband called in my mother to stay with us for the last two weeks of the semester to help at home, and then I left my two small children *during Christmas* to go to New Jersey and stay with my mom, with no obligations to do anything whatsoever. That's how depleted my restoration coffers were.

So, what does restoration mean? Restoration can simply mean rest. When I was trying to make it through the end of the post-Maria year, I would make myself lie down when I got home from work each weekday. I didn't try to cook fancy dinners (my family could eat cereal and survive) or help kids with homework (they were fine on their own). The kids might end up sitting on me or I might find myself watching Dora the Explorer, but that was fine. During the weekends, I set no goals: laundry could pile up, we could eat pasta and jars of sauce for every meal, and the house remained dirty. I needed to squeeze as much rest into my week as possible until the end of the semester when I could turn off work completely. This prevented me from breaking down in an emergency situation. In none-mergency situations, rest can mean trying to get more sleep at night, napping, dropping your laundry off to be done without you, or preserving your weekend for non-work activities.

Restoration can also mean doing activities that fill you up, so they may not at first appear restful, but they are most definitely restorative. For example, runners might feel energized and less stressed after a run. I love walking to calm down and reset my brain. I also use page-turning young adult novels to help fill my cup and restore my mind. Building these kinds of activities into your days and weeks can help you honor the create/restore relationship so that you protect your creative abilities and avoid that "lack of motivation" feeling.

This is all to say that if you feel a lack of motivation, you might simply need restoration. But lack of motivation is also a natural, normal, expected state for people whose job is essentially one of creation. You create courses and lectures, publications and grants, committee reports and curricula; expecting to remain equally motivated throughout it all is, again, oppressive. You are not a machine, and your amount of "production" will increase and decrease as you ride the ebbs and flows of the semester and deal with derailing events. That's okay. Because you have a sustainable, relationship-based writing system, you can ride it out.

Rebellious Reflection:

1. What are the predictable activities that take over (grading, travel, etc.) your calendar?

2. When do they occur?

3. What could you do to predict ebbs and flows and build in gentleness?

4. What are the typical "academic derailments" that you experience? Make a list, then build systems and processes for dealing with each one.

Chapter 8:
The Role of Rest in Writing

I ended the last chapter by making the connection between motivation and rest. Having worked with hundreds of academic womxn and nonbinary people over the last five years as a coach and spent twenty years as an academic myself, I know that telling academics to rest often falls on deaf ears. The immediate response to a suggestion of rest is, "I don't have time."

I would be doing all of you readers a great disservice if I didn't emphasize the relationship between rest and writing. In fact, for many of you, this may be *the* missing piece in creating the career and life you want. Writing needs rest. In this chapter, I'm digging into not only why but how to make rest a part of your writing practice.

The culture of academia is not set up to value rest. We push undone to-dos into the semester and summer breaks. There is an expectation that we will "catch up" whenever we have time off. When we do rest, we often feel guilty for doing so. A client posted about feeling guilty for working on a revise and resubmit on Mother's Day and then again feeling guilty later that day when she stopped writing to have dinner with her family. Time "off" feels like a no-win situation.

In the previous chapter, I mentioned Natalie Miller, who taught me about the relationship between creation and restoration. We were at a business retreat in a beautiful home on the North Carolina coast. Snuggled into a big sectional couch while it rained outside, a handful of business owners and I watched Natalie draw a lemniscate on a flip chart (an infinity symbol, or a number eight on its side). I remember her labeling one side "creation" and the other "restoration" and then traced her marker over and over the lemniscate, back and forth. "If you want to create more," she said, making the creation side a little bigger, "you need to restore more." And she circled through the restore side of the lemniscate, making it a little bigger. We are socialized to think that if we want to create more, we should spend more time creating. "But that makes the lemniscate lopsided," Natalie explained, drawing a new symbol where the creation loop was five times bigger than the restoration loop. It feels counterintuitive in our work-obsessed culture, but in that moment, Natalie convinced me that to increase creation, we need to increase restoration.

As I was writing this chapter, I called Natalie to ask her where this idea of the create/restore cycle came from

(I wanted to cite my sources, of course!). Turns out, I had gotten it wrong. The two sides of Natalie's lemniscate were actually creation/integration, which is an adaptation of Martha Beck's creation/play version. In a chain of adaptation for our coaching audiences, I had remembered and taught my coaching clients the create/restore cycle, with an emphasis on restoration as rest. I think I remembered create/restore instead of create/integrate because that's what academic writers need. My brain unconsciously adapted Natalie's idea to my own experience. But the core ideas are the same: pouring all your time and energy into creation without also pouring into restoration (or integration or play) backfires, but we are conditioned to think otherwise. We are conditioned to work five days a week and rest for two, work all year for a two week vacation, and take an eight-week unpaid maternity leave. None of the norms of Northwestern society (the society that academia centers) acknowledge the cost of creation, which must be paid in restoration.

Your work as an academic is ultimately creative work. We may think of painters and composers as creators. Novel writers qualify as well. But academics? Academic writing? It is not categorized as creation, but it absolutely, positively *is*.

Most of what you do all day is create new things. You create lesson plans and lectures. You create new scholars as you mentor students. You create millions of dollars in grant funding from a few pages of a proposal. You create knowledge through your research. And writing up that knowledge is absolutely an act of creation.

Here's the thing about the relationship between creation and restoration. We think that to create more (write more, get more grants, graduate more PhD students), we need to spend more time creating. But as Natalie illustrated that day with the lopsided lemniscate, to create more, we need to attend to restoration. This is not to say that the purpose of restoring yourself is *only* to create more but rather that an appropriate amount of restoration is absolutely essential for creation, and most academics are so depleted that they are on the verge of stopping their creation entirely (i.e., burning out). Because we operate within a culture that doesn't value rest, most of us don't even know where to start implementing a plan for restoring more.

Let me be clear: understanding the connection between creation and restoration and taking action to restore more is not optional.

If you implement my advice for creating a writing system, honoring your boundaries, and putting writing at the center of your career, but you ignore this part, you will fail.

Rest is not optional for writers. And *you* are a writer!

Alex Soojung-Kim Pang, in his book *Rest: Why You Get More Done When You Work Less*, argues that "work and rest are partners."[28] He goes on to say that work and rest are not opposites, as post-industrial-revolution culture would lead us to believe. Nor is rest the absence of work. Like the infinity symbol, the two are connected, intertwined, in relationship. Pang uses a wave metaphor, saying work and rest are "more like different points on life's wave. You can't have a crest without a trough. You can't have the highs without the lows. Neither can exist without each other."[29] Pang's point in advocating for and describing the relationship between work and rest is not to increase productivity. Instead, he advocates rest to feed the creativity that is your life's work, that makes you happy and fulfilled. "When we stop and rest properly, we're not paying a tax on creativity. We're investing in it."[30] In other words, work needs rest.

In *The Art of Rest: How To Find Respite In The Modern Age*, Claudia Hammond argues that if we are constantly "busy," a claim that so many academics wear as a badge of honor, "life lacks essential rhythm. We miss out on the contrasts between doing and not doing. This oscillation is natural and healthy."[31] Hammond envisions this work/rest relationship as a hammock, swinging back and forth.

Whether we envision the relationship between work and rest as a lemniscate, a wave, or a hammock swinging in the breeze, all the metaphors conclude they are connected. Work and rest feed off each other.

The Concept of "Deliberate Rest"

Rest is not simply the absence of work, as Pang notes. When I had toddler-aged children, evenings and weekends at home felt like more "work" than weekdays at the university, even though I wasn't grading papers or doing anything related to my profession. Even now that my children are older, being with them is fun and rewarding, but it is not restful. In other words, resting from the work of being a professor by doing other kinds of work—caregiving, housework, etc.—is not good enough to expand the restoration part of the create/restore cycle. We need more than simply "not working our professor job" to get the increased creation that comes from pouring into restoration.

Rest can be strenuous physical activity for some people, or it can be sedentary and still. Hammond defines rest simply as "any restful activity that we do while we're awake."[32] Likewise, Pang argues that rest is active, that "physical activity is more restful than we expect, and mental rest is more active than we realize."[33] In my experience with necessary rest after disruptions in my life (particularly after hurricane Maria, which I talked about in an earlier chapter), I found that I needed what Pang calls "deliberate rest." Simply put, deliberate rest is rest on purpose. At the end of the school year of Maria, I made a plan for rest. It was not a very complicated plan, but it was absolutely deliberate.

Restorative rest is thoughtfully designed. Pang argues it's also a skill. We need to get good at it! And if you are an overworked academic, you probably aren't very good at rest—yet. In fact, you may still be resistant to the idea.

Before I dig into *how* to rest to restore, I'm going to tackle the most common oppositions to rest that I hear from my academic clients. See if you hear yourself in any of these anti-rest oppositions.

Opposition to Rest

As I mentioned at the beginning of this chapter, the most common opposition to rest that I hear from my academic writing coaching clients is: "I don't have time to rest." Of course, it feels that way. We are conditioned to feel time scarcity in academia, and if we can let writing fall to the bottom of the list, rest isn't even on our radar. But remember what you learned about scarcity and abundance way back in the second chapter. A scarcity mindset drives us to make decisions based on fear—in this case, the fear is that if we rest, we will run out of time for all the other tasks we need to do each day.

But wait, don't you already feel like you don't have enough time to get everything done? Isn't that fear already true right now?

If your fear about resting is that you won't get as much done as you want, and now you know that to create more you need to restore more, then you have nothing to lose by trying rest. No one is going to magically add hours to your day for restoring yourself. You must make strategic decisions about how to use your time to achieve your goals. And if writing is one of your goals, then rest is not optional. Remember that the two go hand in hand.

Overworked academics also tell me they can't rest because taking a break is more stressful than just working through their list. This thought pattern goes against pretty much everything we know about productivity. As you push through a need to rest, the quality of your work diminishes. All hours spent in front of the computer are not created equal.

Remember the concept of soaring versus slogging? You can get more done soaring than you can in the same amount of time slogging. Way more. When you completely embrace this concept, you no longer will feel that taking a break is more stressful than working through your list. When you start to see the impact of using your Soaring State and avoiding your Slogging State, you will break up with the idea that all hours of work are equally valuable.

The concept that taking a break is more stressful than just pushing through sets you up for burnout. It embraces a binge-and-burn approach to your work: you binge-work hours and hours, pushing through rest and slogging along, which inevitably leads to a crash, and you can't work at all. "Just pushing through" might temporarily ease your mind, which has been conditioned to believe that the way to get more done is to work more hours, but it will not help you reach your desired outcome in the long run. Your capacity to create is linked to your capacity to restore, and the more you binge and burn, the more you are denying yourself the ability to take advantage of the create/restore cycle.

Closely linked to the idea that taking a break is more stressful than just pushing through is believing that if you take a break you will get (further) behind. There is no end destination for academic work. If you have a belief about where you "should" be, based on comparing yourself (apples to oranges) to where you perceive others to be, you are playing a comparison game that you will never win. Constantly feeling behind is eating away at your ability to create.

You get to decide where you should be. You get to decide which projects get priority and which tasks to shed to focus on what matters to you and your career. There is no "behind."

Guilt surrounding rest may be the biggest opposition most academics I work with have to restoring themselves. The culture of overwork and the nature of academia make us believe that we could—and should—be working all the time, from anywhere. If we take a break, we feel guilty for leaving the work. But the opposite also holds: if we work more, we feel guilty for neglecting our friends, our loved ones, and ourselves. Guilt is not only the biggest killer of writing momentum but it also puts you in a no-win situation.

When you are plagued by guilt if you *do* work and guilt if you *don't* work, guilt is paralyzing. There is no upside to guilt. I don't want you to make decisions based on fear, but at least fear lights a fire to get something done. Guilt dampens everything and creates a downward spiral of lost faith in yourself. The solution, of course, is restoration. The way out of a guilt spiral is not to work more; it is to rest more.

How to Rest to Restore

I hope by now you're convinced of the value of rest, but I know many academics work so hard that they don't even know where to start when they finally decide to rest.

Claudia Hammond and her team surveyed 18,000 people with an instrument called The Rest Test. In her book, *The Art of Rest*, she reviews the top ten restful activities that the survey revealed. They are a mix of active and passive activities, including: mindfulness, watching TV, and daydreaming as well as a good walk and spending time in nature. Some activities that did not make the top ten included time with family and friends and browsing social media.

When you are creating deliberate rest for yourself, you are not simply looking for an absence of work, and you are not looking to replace one kind of work (academic) with another kind of work (household). Instead, Hammond argues, "To get top quality rest you need to work out which are the essential elements of life that contribute most to you achieving a sense of restfulness."[34] Just like developing your writing practice involves self-reflection, so does creating your restorative practice.

Once you've figured out the kinds of activities that are most restful to you, you have to schedule them. Hammond suggests putting breaks in your calendar just like you put appointments. Some amount of rest should happen every single day, whether it's a fifteen-minute walk or an hour spent reading a novel. Create rhythms for yourself, like Pang's wave. These rhythms can be hourly, like a twenty-five-minute-write/five-minute break. They can be daily, like a lunchtime walk across campus, or weekly, with more rest happening on the weekend.

If you feel like you often find yourself "wasting time" or "procrastinating," perhaps you are actually trying to create these necessary create/restore rhythms. Instead of resisting them, judging yourself, and feeling guilty, lean in. Figure out how best you like to rest and instead of "procrastinating" by piddling around your office or scrolling social media, lean into deliberate rest and read a book or even daydream. The point is that restoring yourself is essential for the creation you are trying to accomplish in your writing, so turning your brain and body's yearning for rest into a deliberate practice is essential to your growth as an academic writer.

Rebellious Reflections:

1. What active rest is most restorative for you?
2. What passive rest is most restorative for you?
3. How can you incorporate both active and passive rest into your workday?
4. Your work week?
5. Your year?

Conclusion:
Writing as Transformation

In 1975, Dan Lortie coined the term "apprenticeship of observation" to refer to the phenomenon whereby future teachers begin teacher education programs having participated in thousands of hours of observation of teachers as schoolchildren. The result is a notion of what it takes to be a professional teacher that is highly influenced by those hours and hours of observation. Academic careers are learned through an apprenticeship of observation. This is unlike trainees in many other professions. For example, doctors may have spent only a handful of hours in contact with doctors in action before entering medical school. The apprenticeship of observation can make innovation in teacher education slow and difficult, as would-be teachers must unlearn what thousands of hours of the apprenticeship of observation has taught them.

The apprenticeship of observation applies to academic careers beyond teaching as well. We spend hours and hours as students observing college professors during our bachelor's, master's, and doctoral programs. We see professors in classrooms, in laboratories, and in individual meetings about our research work, but we never see how those professors manage their careers behind-the-scenes. All we learn about career management we divine from the outside. This makes academia particularly vulnerable to reproducing cultural norms that are not necessarily the ones that will lead to an enriching professional experience. But we've never seen another way, so we replicate the way that we've seen.

We know that academic culture needs to change, but how can we achieve that?

Throughout this book I've talked about writing as a metaphor for a larger way of existing in the academic world. That's because I truly believe that a focus on writing can be the driver of the cultural change needed in academia.

When we focus on writing, we necessarily focus on ourselves, our work, and our time. Writing serves as an organizer for not only career change but also for the personal and professional development that asks us to hold boundaries, release guilt, create calm, and manage our time to our best advantage. This is a book about making time to write. But it is more deeply a book about using the goal of making time to write to transform yourself and your career.

I believe that this individual transformation is essential for the cultural transformation of academia. Trained as an ethnographer, I'm obsessed with everyday practices—the small, recurring events driven by our deep beliefs that, in sum, add up to culture. Changes to writing practices—the choice to make and keep a date with your writing just once a week, for example—add up to larger cultural changes. And though systemic changes absolutely must also occur, as a trained linguistic anthropologist, I am in love with the power of tiny changes distributed amongst many people that can topple whole systems by shifting their very foundations.

If all academic womxn and nonbinary people stopped scheduling last-minute committee meetings over their writing times and started saying, "No, I can't meet then; that's my writing time," writing appointments could take on the cultural importance of doctor's appointments. And why not? The beliefs around which types of appointments can be canceled and which must be honored are culturally constructed. So, let's construct something new, something that serves us.

Seth Godin defines culture with the simple phrase: *People like us do things like this*. Translate that into academic culture and we get: *Academics like us do things like this*. Academics like us publish in the top journals, bring in the big money, and mentor the best students.

If that is what academic culture is, it is also: Academics like us work nights and weekends, burn out before tenure, get bullied by ruthless colleagues, and idolize overwork.

That's not the academic culture I want. That is the culture we must change with our everyday actions.

I want to create a culture in which academics like us are driven by purpose and deep calling, support each other in difficult times, and celebrate each other's successes. One where academics like us write and publish more, work *and* rest, take care of ourselves and others. Womxn and nonbinary people will be thriving in academia when academics like us know that deep work is important, know that our institution values our deep work, and know that students want to learn what we can uniquely teach.

People like us do things like this.

Cultural change is simple, but not easy.

Real cultural change in academia will happen through a ripple effect. You will take what you learned in this book and start to implement it. It won't be perfect, and you might have to come back here and reread to remind yourself of the mindset and practical shifts that you intend to make right now. The pull to rely on familiar practices and beliefs, the ones ingrained in you powerfully by years and years in the apprenticeship of observation, will undermine your excitement for what you've read here. You will default to overwork, permeable boundaries, and taking on too much. But just by trying, even if it takes many tries to make the things I talk about in this book stick, you are sending powerful ripples into the world. You are changing what is taught in the apprenticeship of observation as others observe *you*.

Ripples of Change

In the first chapter of this book, I situated your individual experience as a writer in the context of the racist, ableist patriarchal culture of academia. I tried to shift the blame for womxn and nonbinary academics struggling to make time to write away from the individual and onto the cultural.

Letting writing fall to the bottom of the list or sacrificing nights and weekends to overflowing amounts of work is not the fault of individual people. The fault lies with the culture in which we are operating and the way in which we are socialized in that culture. I dug deeper into this idea in the second chapter, in which I introduced the twin scarcities that are a result of academic culture: scarcity of time and scarcity of money. Those scarcities cause us to (logically) operate from a place of fear in our decision-making about writing. I suggested that we don't have to continue to make those fear-based decisions. Even though we are socialized within a culture of academia that causes us to develop certain beliefs, we are not without agency to react to that culture differently. We can make decisions based on an abundance mindset, even within real-world conditions (and perceived conditions) of scarcity.

And that is the crux of it: we are products of the culture of academia, but we are not defined by how that culture has socialized us. Nor can we wait for systemic changes to have the careers and lives we want. Systemic change and individual change must happen simultaneously. Real, lasting change is cocreated by both.

This book is about individual change, but that change is always contextualized within the culture we uncovered in the first two chapters. Chapters 3–8 walked you through the kinds of individual changes you can make to make time to write. I talked about soaring versus slogging and how to build your days around your writing. I wrote about what you really need when you think you need account-ability (community!) and how your inner dialogue about what you "should" do is based on false assumptions about what everyone else is doing. I emphasized that predict-ability—really knowing yourself and how long it takes *you* to do things—is more valuable than speed. And finally, I reframed lack of motivation as a natural reaction to both predictable and unpredictable disruptions in your writ-ing practice and emphasized the role of rest in recovering from those derailments. I explained how creation and res-toration are linked; therefore, rest is essential to writing.

All these new ways of doing and thinking that add up to more writing are individual changes, performed in the context of an oppressive culture. It won't be easy to try them (you've probably resisted a lot of what I suggest in this book), and it won't be easy to maintain them consid-ering the cultural forces that want you to stay overworked and exhausted—and silent. But as you do them anyway (because you *can* do very, very hard things), those around you are changed as your ripples of change become waves. The apprentices observing you setting boundaries, cen-tering your writing, and designing the career you want on your terms will take those observations with them as they design *their* careers. Your individual changes cause cultural shifts.

In the End, Though, It's Okay to Just Change You

I've said on my podcast that knowledge-making needs diverse voices; it needs the voices of marginalized people, of Black, Brown, and Indigenous people. I've said that humanity loses when those voices are silenced. And that's all true. But that's not why I want womxn and nonbinary people to make time to write.

I want you to make time to write because you deserve to have the career you want. It is important that you—individual you—thrive in academia, for no other reason than that you want to.

Don't worry about being an example for those coming up if that feels overwhelming or hard. It is absolutely good enough to focus entirely on yourself and your own writing and career without worrying about cultural change. Even if the changes that you make after reading this book never affect anyone else, they are important because *you* enjoying *your career* is important.

In the end, it's okay to just change you.

About the Author

Cathy Mazak was a tenured, full professor and mom of three when she founded a writing-centered professional development company for academics. Cathy and her team help womxn and nonbinary professors find time to write, publish work they love, and design their careers on their terms. She has a PhD from Michigan State University and is the editor of several scholarly collections and the author of numerous textbooks and academic journal articles. In her work as a professor at The University of Puerto Rico, Mayagüez, she attracted external funding for her work in bilingualism and higher education and co-founded a research center. Her popular podcast, *Academic Writing Amplified*, teaches listeners how to use writing to resist the racist, ableist, patriarchal culture of academia. Cathy lives in Mayagüez, Puerto Rico.

Endnotes

1   Joanne L. Bagshaw, PhD, *The Feminist Handbook,* (Canada: Raincoast Books, 2019).

2   Joanne L. Bagshaw, PhD, *The Feminist Handbook,* (Canada: Raincoast Books, 2019).

3   George Yancy and bell hooks, "bell hooks: Buddhism, the Beats and Loving Blackness," *The New York Times* (December 10, 2015), https://opinionator.blogs. nytimes.com/author/bell-hooks/.

4   Kimberle Crenshaw, "Mapping the Margins: Intersectionality, Identity Politics, and Violence against Women of Color," Stanford Law Review, 43(6), 1241- 1299, (1991), doi:10.2307/1229039.

5   S. Bae, "Hxrstory of WRRC," (September 27, 2018), Retrieved October 19, 2020, from https://wrrc.ucdavis.edu/about/hxrstory.

6   S. Bae, "Hxrstory of WRRC," (September 27, 2018), Retrieved October 19, 2020, from https://wrrc.ucdavis.edu/about/hxrstory.

7   W. C. Byrd, R.J. Brunn-Bevel, & S.M. Ovink, *Intersectionality and Higher Education: Identity and inequal-*

ity on college campuses, (New Brunswick: Rutgers University Press, 2019).

8   Glenn Colby and Chelsea Fowler, "Data Snapshot: IPEDS Data on Full-Time Women Faculty and Faculty of Color," American Association of University Professors, (December 2020), https://www.aaup.org/sites/default/files/Dec-2020_Data_Snapshot_Women_and_Faculty_of_Color.pdf.

9   Catalyst, "Women in Academia: Quick Take," (January 23, 2020), Retrieved October 19, 2020, from https://www.catalyst.org/research/women-in-academia/.

10   American Association of University Professors, "The Annual Report on the Economic Status of the Profession, 2018-19," https://www.aaup.org/report/annual-report-economic-status-profession-2018-19.

11   Jessica Gullion, "Scholar, Negated," in *Mama, PhD*, ed. E. Evans and C. Grant (New Brunswick: Rutgers University Press, 2008).

12   Francie Diep, "'I Was Fed Up': How #BlackInTheIvory Got Started, and What Its Founders Want to See Next," The Chronicle of Higher Education (June 9, 2020), https://www.chronicle.com/article/i-was-fed-up-how-blackintheivory-got-started-and-what-its-founders-want-to-see-next.

13   https://www.citeblackwomencollective.org/

14   Henry A. Giroux, *Neoliberalism's War on Higher Education*, (Chicago, IL: Haymarket Books, 2020).

15 R.J. Brunn-Bevel, S. M. Ovink, W.C. Byrd, and A.D. Mahoney, "Always crossing boundaries, always existing in multiple bubbles: Intersected experiences and positions on college campuses," in *Intersectionality in Higher Education*, ed. W.A. Carson, R.J. Brunn-Bevel, and S.M. Ovink, (New Brunswick: Rutgers UP, 2019), 9.

16 Colleen Flaherty, "Early journal submission data suggest COVID-19 is tanking women's research productivity," Inside Higher Ed (April 21, 2020), Retrieved October 19, 2020, from https://www.insidehighered.com/news/2020/04/21/early-journal-submission-data-suggest-covid-19-tanking-womens-research-productivity.

17 Andrea R. Jain, "An Update on Journal Publishing and a Plea for our Discipline in the Time of Pandemic," American Academy of Religion, Retrieved from https://www.aarweb.org/AARMBR/Publications-and-News-/Newsroom-/News-/An-Update-on-Journal-Publishing-and-a-Plea-for-our-Discipline-in-the-Time-of-Pandemic.aspx?fbclid=IwAR1lpquv9uY-rjHUimRE3GEZRQszku-8Do8D66BpjgKZTYtE_AqBySOXdFYg.

18 Social Sciences Feminist Research Interest Group, 2017.

19 Maggie Berg and Barbara K. Seeber, *The Slow Professor*, (Toronto: University of Toronto Press, 2017), 2–3.

20 Maggie Berg and Barbara K. Seeber, *The Slow Professor*, (Toronto: University of Toronto Press, 2017), 2.

21 Maggie Berg and Barbara K. Seeber, *The Slow Professor*, (Toronto: University of Toronto Press, 2017), 5.

22 Kevin Carey, "The Bleak Job Landscape of Adjunctopia for Ph.Ds," *New York Times*, Retrieved from https://www.nytimes.com/2020/03/05/upshot/academic-job-crisis-phd.html.

23 Tara Mohr, *Playing Big*, (New York: Gotham Books, 2014), 65.

24 Tara Mohr, *Playing Big*, (New York: Gotham Books, 2014), 66.

25 Michaeleen Doucleff, "Rate Of C-Sections Is Rising At An 'Alarming' Rate, Report Says," NPR (October 12, 2018), Retrieved from https://www.npr.org/sections/goatsandsoda/2018/10/12/656198429/rate-of-c-sections-is-rising-at-an-alarming-rate.

26 Tara Mohr, *Playing Big*, (New York: Gotham Books, 2014), 44.

27 http://www.alexandrafranzen.com/2018/07/12/go-with-your-hut/

28 Alex Soojung-Kim Pang, *Rest*, (New York: Basic Books, 2018, 11.

29 Alex Soojung-Kim Pang, *Rest*, (New York: Basic Books, 2018, 3.

30 Alex Soojung-Kim Pang, *Rest*, (New York: Basic Books, 2018, 11.

31 Claudia Hammond, *The Art of Rest*, (Edinburgh: Cannongate Press, 2019), 2.

32 Claudia Hammond, *The Art of Rest*, (Edinburgh: Cannongate Press, 2019), 7.

33 Alex Soojung-Kim Pang, *Rest*, (New York: Basic Books, 2018, 12.

34 Claudia Hammond, *The Art of Rest*, (Edinburgh: Cannongate Press, 2019), 251.

A free ebook edition is available with the purchase of this book.

To claim your free ebook edition:

1. Visit MorganJamesBOGO.com
2. Sign your name CLEARLY in the space
3. Complete the form and submit a photo of the entire copyright page
4. You or your friend can download the ebook to your preferred device

Print & Digital Together Forever.

Snap a photo   Free ebook   Read anywhere